PENGUIN BOOKS

SOMETHING HAPPENED ON THE WAY TO HEAVEN

Sudha Murty was born in 1950 in Shiggaon in north Karnataka. She did her MTech in computer science, and is now the chairperson of the Infosys Foundation. A prolific writer in English and Kannada, she has written novels, technical books, travelogues, collections of short stories and non-fictional pieces, and four books for children. Her books have been translated into all the major Indian languages.

Sudha Murty was the recipient of the R.K. Narayan Award for Literature and the Padma Shri in 2006, and the Attimabbe Award from the government of Karnataka for excellence in Kannada literature in 2011.

Also by Sudha Murty

FICTION
Dollar Bahu
Mahashweta
Gently Falls the Bakula
House of Cards
The Mother I Never Knew: Two Novellas

NON-FICTION
Wise and Otherwise
The Old Man and His God
The Day I Stopped Drinking Milk

CHILDREN'S FICTION
*How I Taught My Grandmother to Read and
Other Stories*
The Magic Drum and Other Favourite Stories
The Bird with Golden Wings: Stories of Wit and Magic
Grandma's Bag of Stories

SUDHA MURTY

SOMETHING HAPPENED
ON THE WAY TO HEAVEN

20 Inspiring Real-Life Stories

PENGUIN BOOKS

PENGUIN BOOKS
Published by the Penguin Group
Penguin Books India Pvt. Ltd, 7th Floor, Infinity Tower C, DLF Cyber City,
Gurgaon 122 002, Haryana, India
Penguin Group (USA) Inc., 375 Hudson Street, New York, New York 10014, USA
Penguin Group (Canada), 90 Eglinton Avenue East, Suite 700, Toronto,
Ontario, M4P 2Y3, Canada
Penguin Books Ltd, 80 Strand, London WC2R 0RL, England
Penguin Ireland, 25 St Stephen's Green, Dublin 2, Ireland
(a division of Penguin Books Ltd)
Penguin Group (Australia), 707 Collins Street, Melbourne, Victoria 3008, Australia
Penguin Group (NZ), 67 Apollo Drive, Rosedale, Auckland 0632, New Zealand
Penguin Books (South Africa) (Pty) Ltd, Block D, Rosebank Office Park,
181 Jan Smuts Avenue, Parktown North, Johannesburg 2193, South Africa

Penguin Books Ltd, Registered Offices: 80 Strand, London WC2R 0RL, England

First published by Penguin Books India 2014

10 9 8 7 6 5

ISBN 9780143423928

Typeset in Sabon LT Std by Eleven Arts, Delhi
Printed at Thomson Press India Ltd, New Delhi

A PENGUIN RANDOM HOUSE COMPANY

Contents

Contents

Introduction

One day, shortly after the release of my last book in the market, I was on my way home from work when I thought about my unexpected literary journey. I was filled with awe as I realized that the books I've been able to write are really not about me at all—they are about the people I've met, the places I've been to and the lives I've had the privilege of being a part of. I felt blessed—so fortunate to be in a position to help people, even as they found it in their hearts to let me inside their world and share their most private thoughts and problems with me. They've given me their stories and I've had a chance to be a character in their tales. Sometimes, I've been lucky enough to be the lead actor, but at most other times, I've been an incidental character or simply the unbiased storyteller.

So when I sat down to discuss this book with Shrutkeerti Khurana, my wonderful and trusted editor, and Udayan Mitra, my publisher at Penguin, I wanted to do something different. For many years, writing has been a one-way street from me to you, the reader. You connect with me because we share the same values and we are both fascinated with the varied facets of the human mind. This time, I hoped for a chance to reach out to you and all my readers more fully: I wanted to learn from the experiences life has gifted *you*. So we came up with the idea for a contest and requested our readers to send in inspiring real-life stories. I'm so pleased that we did, because the untold stories we discovered simply swept us off our feet.

Inside this book, the storytellers will take you to places that will restore your faith in today's youth and make you admire their courage to tell the truth like it is. A girl called Aagneya will capture your heart and make you wish that she were your daughter, even if she did something that society judges to be terribly wrong.

Then there's a story about a boy who stands bravely by his Alzheimer's-stricken and violent grandfather. Even a group of impoverished children who pick fallen fruit off the streets after a storm have an important life lesson to teach us.

As we read and re-read the wonderful submissions we received, we found that the older generation still has some tricks up their sleeves when it comes to parenting and handling tricky life situations. There's a father who just can't seem to find his glasses, an elderly school principal who sends a bad man running with his tail between his legs, and a mysterious couple who get adopted by a little girl. A young man understands the true nature of love when he sees a rare moment of truth between his aged and bedridden grandparents, and another realizes just how much respect his grandfather, a schoolteacher, still commands after decades have gone by.

I hope that some of the stories will give you goosebumps, just like I got when we read about a woman hiring a eunuch as her housemaid, a bunch of 'goondas' protecting a young girl on a dark and rainy night, a plastic surgeon refusing to operate on patients demanding unnecessary procedures, and the poignant story of a boy who, decades ago, saved a baby langur from certain death.

Then you'll learn about the great escape of a girl from the monkey tribe, a beautiful woman who refuses to back down after she is acid-attacked, a single mother who survives an almost-fatal building fire, and a young woman who shows great resilience when she is attacked on a train. The women of today are not looking for sympathy, pity or charity. They are looking for change—a change in the mindset, and the implementation of the laws of the land, which are just and fair. What they probably don't know is that they themselves are the harbingers of a change that is long overdue.

There's a saying that fact is stranger than fiction. Fiction stems from imagination and there is a limit to what we can imagine. But in real life—there really is no end to where we might go and what our experiences might have to teach us, is there? Human stories about escape from a nightmarish situation during Partition, a housemaid who invests everything in educating her daughter, an adoption that changes an entire family's life, and a person who lives by the principle of 'paying it forward' brought me to tears, sometimes of sadness but mostly of joy.

I grow older with each year that passes by and sometimes it becomes just a little difficult to retain my faith in humanity. The stories in this book, which were chosen from over a thousand stories that we received, have affirmed to me that there is still more good than bad in this world and more love than hate. I hope you will enjoy these stories as much as I did, and that they will inspire you like they inspired me.

Sudha Murty

Acceptance

by Bhaswar Mukherjee

The January sun streamed in mercilessly at 7 a.m. through the open window on the seventh floor, into the Srinivasan household in Mylapore. With three principal seasons in Chennai—hot, hotter and hottest—the city was already warm in a month that was still winter in most parts of the country.

In tandem, the temperatures within the household were reaching boiling point too. The concatenation of events started with Mr Ashoke Srinivasan's mother's visit to Chennai during the auspicious Pongal festival, which traditionally signalled the onset of the harvest with prayers for agricultural abundance. Savitri had painstakingly and lovingly brought the choicest savouries and sweets for her son and her grandson Vijay, a three-year-old toddler. Her relationship with her daughter-in-law Rama was cold at best and hostile at worst. Savitri grudged Rama's rather modern upbringing in Delhi and had continued to berate her husband Srinivasan Vellu for the match till Mr Vellu passed on to the next world. Savitri was left behind to fend for herself and jostle for space and acceptance within her son's world which was rapidly moving away from her—first with his marriage and then with the arrival of his child.

A further reason for the raised mercury levels was the fact that just a few days ago, the household's live-in maid had demanded a week's vacation during the festival. When it was not forthcoming, she had quit her job in a huff. Now, there was no one to take care of Vijay. Rama was clear that they would not take unfair advantage of Savitri's visit; the family needed a long-term solution for domestic support.

But then Rama's request for some days off from work to handle the crisis at home had also been declined.

In the living room, Ashoke was immersed in *The Hindu*—the staple diet of news for the city. He was engrossed in an article that was lobbying for the recognition of and equal opportunities for transgender people as the legitimate third sex.

Suddenly, Rama cursed under her breath and slammed down a tumbler of coffee on the table next to Ashoke. Sensing her anger and frustration, he attempted to douse the fire. 'Calm down, Rama, we will work something out,' he said, putting the newspaper aside and reaching for the coffee.

Rama, who had already turned to go, spun back. She put her hands on her hips and glared at him, panting slightly, her bosom heaving with the turmoil of emotions. She was perspiring from the strain of cooking and attending to the morning chores.

Jallikattu is a bull-taming sport popular in Tamil Nadu as a part of the Pongal celebrations. Unlike the Spanish running of the bulls, the animals here are neither killed, nor does the 'matador' use any weapons. The bulls are picked predominantly from the Pulikulam breed of cattle, which attacks not because they are irritated or agitated or frightened, but because that is their basic nature. Those daring to tame the bulls adopt strategies of either 'fight' or 'flight'. It was with similar trepidation that Ashoke met Rama's eyes.

'How? How will we ever work anything out if you are more involved with the affairs of the state than with those of your own home?' she demanded.

'What about the agency we had tried earlier . . .?' offered Ashoke weakly.

'They sent us two and a half maids over three months.'

'Half?' he countered, quite forgetting that silence was the better part of valour in arguments with his wife.

'Don't you remember anything?' thundered Rama. 'They sent us someone almost as young as Vijay!'

Hearing the commotion in the living room, Savitri stopped decorating the foyer with the traditional kolam and came rushing in with Vijay in tow. 'What happened, Ashoke?' she asked as she closed the door and wiped her stained hands on her sari.

Rama turned to look at Savitri with her eyes blazing. Mother- and daughter-in-law locked eyes with each other, almost as if daring the other to advance proceedings.

Vijay, who had previously been squatting next to Savitri in the foyer watching her draw intricate patterns with coloured rice powder on the floor, sensed the lack of parental attention and started sucking on the piece of chalk in his hand.

And as often happens in the battle between royals, the poor rookie pawn is sacrificed. 'Vijay!' Rama shrieked as her son helped himself to a generous chunk of limestone. He immediately dropped the chalk and started bawling.

The melee was interrupted by the doorbell. On most mornings, the doorbell was unwelcome because the family was busy trying to rush off to work or school. Today, however, it had a salubrious effect. Vijay stopped mid-bawl and the fight went out of Savitri and Rama who withdrew their claws. Ashoke looked at the door with the gratitude of a losing pugilist at the sound of the end-of-bout bell.

Rama opened the door and was taken aback. An enormous lady stood there. She was dressed in an ill-fitting sari and towered close to six feet with long and muscular arms. With sudden shock, Rama realized that the person in front of her resembled the many eunuchs who roamed the streets of the city, stopping traffic and asking for money. 'Do these people now have the temerity to leave the streets and come knocking at our doors?' she wondered.

Deciding to exercise caution rather than display annoyance, she closed the door just enough to engage the night lock and asked stiffly, 'Yes? What is it?'

The lady said politely in a man's voice, 'I'm sorry to disturb you, Ma'am. I heard that you are looking for a maid. Is that true?'

Rama remembered the aggression that these marginalized creations of God often exhibited in public by clapping their hands in her face or knocking on the car window and demanding money. She was taken aback by the politeness.

'We . . . we . . .' she floundered.

Her response was cut short by a shriek in her ear. Savitri's curiosity had got the better of her and she was next to Rama. 'Shut the door! Shut the door!' she screamed.

'Just wait here . . .' Rama managed to say before hastily closing the door.

Savitri ran to Ashoke and cried, 'There is a man at the door dressed as a woman. He's come to rob us! What should we do? Should we call the police?'

Ashoke stood up, abandoning all hope of ever getting through the morning newspaper. It was impossible for a man to read the newspaper in a leisurely fashion as befitted a holiday when accosted by shouting wives and wailing mothers.

Vijay added his might to the chaos by bawling even louder and clinging to Rama.

Rama kneeled down to calm Vijay. Drawing her son to her bosom, she looked up at Ashoke. 'It is strange,' she said in a quiet voice. 'There is a eunuch at the door asking for work as a maid.'

'Are you sure?' asked Ashoke. 'It could just be . . .' Another thought struck him, 'But how the hell has the watchman allowed this creature inside?'

Rama flinched at the use of the word 'creature'. Before she could protest, Savitri positioned herself between her son and Rama. 'What? What is a eunuch?' she demanded.

Ashoke looked at Rama, waiting for her to save him from this delicate predicament.

'Amma, a eunuch is thiru nangai, an aravani,' explained Rama in Tamil.

'Aiyyo, Shiva, Shiva . . .' incanted Savitri. She closed her eyes and rocked back and forth seeking deliverance from the Almighty for this evil intrusion.

'What should we do?' Rama asked her husband.

'Just give her some money and tell her to go away,'

he replied, and added grudgingly, 'you could also give her one of your old saris. After all, it is a festive occasion.'

Grateful for a solution, Rama went to the bedroom. Within a few minutes, she emerged carrying a well-worn sari and money and went to the front door.

When the visitor saw Rama, she quickly got up and dusted herself. She dwarfed Rama by a good foot.

'We are sorry. We do not need a maid. But here's something for you . . .' Rama's voice trailed off as she flinched while handing out the sari and the money.

The eunuch eyed the items but made no move to take them. She looked imploringly at Rama and said, 'Amma, have you already employed someone? The watchman said that there was no maid working here and yet, he would not allow me in. I begged him at first and later threatened him to let me pass. I apologize for my behaviour. We see the hate and fear in everyone's eyes. Often, it gets the better of us,' she said quietly.

'I am sorry, er . . . what's your name?' asked Rama, somewhat chastened.

The eunuch smiled, revealing betel-stained teeth. 'Thank you, Amma. Someone has asked for my name after a long time. My name is Santoshi. Tell me, please, have you given someone the job already?'

Rama could not bring herself to lie, 'No, not really, but . . .'

'Amma,' interrupted Santoshi, 'I see a rare but familiar emotion in your eyes—pity. Please, Amma, if human beings more fortunate than us continue to fear, hate or pity us, then we will remain in the eclipse of society forever. We will continue to beg, coerce people for money or peddle sex for the voyeuristic pleasures of deranged men. We need a hand from people like you, Amma.'

'Arrey, this aravani is a witch. She must know black magic! She is hypnotizing you with her words. Be careful, Rama!' Savitri whispered in her daughter-in-law's ear.

'No, Pati,' said Santoshi, addressing Savitri as grandmother. 'I am not a witch. I was born as a boy to a poor family. When I was two years old, my father was killed in a drunken brawl. And when I was about that old,' she gestured towards wide-eyed Vijay who was standing near them, 'some hoodlums castrated me and forced me to beg for them.' The pain in her eyes was evident as she recalled the trauma. 'Then I became Santoshi,' she finished abruptly.

'Where do you live?' asked Rama, suddenly ashamed of the money and sari she was holding in her hands.

'In the slums beneath the Kotturpuram Bridge,' she replied. 'A few of us are trying to ensure that the poor slum orphans do not suffer the same fate as us. We take them under our wing, give them food and shelter and protect them. But we do not have the means to do this on a long-term basis. We need a steady income and begging is not enough. Please help us, Amma,' said Santoshi, bringing her palms together in supplication.

Then she looked towards Savitri and said, 'Isn't it a shame, Pati? On the one hand, we are considered auspicious and are invited to celebrate the birth of a child, but on the other, we are so cruelly kept on the periphery of human existence for no fault of ours.'

'Enough!' said Savitri. She held Rama by the hand and dragged her inside. 'Are you insane? Why are you talking to that creature for so long when there is so much work to be done? We have to complete the preparations for the puja too. Ashoke, please drive some sense into her!'

The fight seemed to have gone out of Rama. She slowly extricated her hand from Savitri's grip and looked at her husband, 'Can we give her a try, Ashoke?'

'Rama, please use your common sense—think with your head and not your heart,' Ashoke said. 'How can we leave our three-year-old son with this creature? We do not know what its intentions are; it has not been referred to us by an agency that we can fall back on. There are enough rumours of gangs kidnapping small children for ransom or worse. And just think of the social stigma! How will we ever explain this employment to family and friends? I am not in favour of this,' he finished breathlessly.

'Ashoke, please don't call her a "creature". Don't the regular domestic helps who are normal human beings also commit crimes? I don't know how employing her will affect us, so I cannot even begin to imagine the impact of our decision on our friends, family and society. But if educated people like us do not take the first step to bring these souls into the mainstream, who else will? Also, I am desperate. I will lose my job if I have to stay at home, and you too cannot take a leave of absence. Yes, we don't know how Vijay will take to her either . . .' Rama's voice trailed off as she looked around, 'Where *is* Vijay?'

They all glanced at the main door. It was ajar and swinging slightly on its hinges. Vijay was nowhere in sight.

'Vijay!' screamed Rama as she ran out.

There was no one outside the front door. No Vijay. No Santoshi.

Savitri collapsed in a heap in the foyer wailing, 'Oh God! Oh God! I told you Rama, why did you . . .'

But Rama wasn't listening. She stood rooted to the spot by the front door.

Ashoke grabbed his cell phone from the table, scooped up the house keys and barked orders as he rushed out, 'Amma, stay at home and wait by the phone. In case the doorbell rings, remember to put on the chain before you open the door.' He shook Rama out of her stupor and said, 'Take the lift. I am taking the stairs.' Then he ran down the stairs two at a time.

Rama got into the lift shakily. Her journey of seven floors down in the lift seemed unending. Her heart was in her mouth and she felt unsteady as she stepped into the lobby. Moments later, Ashoke joined her, panting heavily. Taking her by the hand, he ran out of the building.

His worst fears were confirmed. There was no one in the porch or in the kids' park. A swing swung lazily, wafted by the breeze. The main gate was unmanned.

'Damn these security guards! Watchman, Watchman!' yelled Ashoke as Rama and he ran towards the gate. Finally, he saw the security guard Bahadur and shouted, 'Have you seen Vijay leave the premises with that lady who forced her way in a short time ago?'

'No, sir,' replied the guard.

'Let's go to the other gate!' said Ashoke and started sprinting to the back of the apartment complex.

Rama began to feel faint as she tried to keep up. Suddenly, she detected a slight movement at the entrance of the building and veered off, shouting, 'Ashoke, come back!'

Santoshi was sitting at the foot of the staircase, holding Vijay to her bosom. She stood up when she saw them coming towards her.

'How dare you?' cried Rama and tried to snatch Vijay away. To her surprise, her son had both his arms around Santoshi's neck and would not let go.

Santoshi explained, 'Amma, I was waiting outside when the child came running out and went straight into the lift. Before I could react, the doors closed and the lift started moving down. I took the stairs and followed the lift all the way. I managed to grab a hold of the boy here in the lobby and then I immediately went up to your apartment. I rang the bell but Pati refused to open the door. I am sorry.'

Ashoke realized that Santoshi and Vijay had probably been going up in the second lift while Rama and he were rushing downstairs. Yet, something about the story didn't seem quite right.

'Why didn't you take the second lift and go down to find Vijay?' he queried. 'And why didn't you tell us?'

Santoshi cast him an incredulous look, 'Sir, I was scared that the child may get off on a random floor and fall down the stairs. I wasn't thinking of what was right and proper. Thankfully, the lift did not stop on any floor but went all the way down.'

Ashoke felt chastened; he looked at Rama and smiled awkwardly. 'I think you have found your domestic help,' he said. 'Let's all go up, shall we? There's still a mountain of work at home!'

Rama turned to Santoshi and said, 'Thank you.

Will you please come upstairs so that we can discuss the terms of your employment?'

Santoshi whispered softly into Vijay's ear. He smiled and stretched out his arms. Rama scooped Vijay up in her arms and held him tightly as she felt the tears well up in her eyes.

As they walked to the lift, Ashoke asked his wife in a hushed tone, 'How did Vijay take to Santoshi so easily? She looks positively formidable and scary!'

Rama replied, 'A child is innocent and trusting. As we grow up, we become sceptics and taking a leap of faith becomes increasingly difficult.' Then she smiled, 'Or maybe Vijay saw his new and strong aunty as his protector. He knew that I would be angry with him for running out of the house!'

Ashoke laughed.

Santoshi respectfully stood behind them at a distance. When the lift came and the family stepped inside, Santoshi heard Rama saying in a raised voice, 'And dear, the best decisions are made with the heart and not the head. Do you think I would have agreed to our marriage if it was the other way round?'

Santoshi smiled.

A Red Rose

by Saurabh Kumar

My grandfather was a cheerful man who loved nothing more than being with his family. When I was little, he would drive over, bringing along rasgullas and pedas for my sister and me. After eating the goodies, the three of us would walk to the nearby bookstore where my sister would buy the latest Nancy Drew adventure. I loved reading Archie comics but was forced to pick up short illustrated volumes of the *Ramayana* as per Grandpa's wishes—I have come to love and treasure these books since.

Grandpa taught me the value of hard work and the importance of trying one's best. 'Those who try never fail,' he used to say. He was always positive about life, and he never uttered a harsh word. In fact, he was quite the opposite of my grandmother, who was always unhappy and made people around her feel the same way too.

Ten years ago, Grandpa started to lose his memory. At first, we ignored it as a common age-related phenomenon, but soon the problem grew worse. He would go out on some work and forget the way home. He would ask the same question over and over again. He would even ask about his father who had been dead for years, 'Where is he? He was here a few minutes ago.'

Still, we failed to recognize the gravity of it all. Like most families, we were caught up in our own lives. Finally, Grandpa's condition couldn't be ignored any more. We took him to a doctor who diagnosed that he was suffering from Alzheimer's disease. We were all stunned. Nobody in our family had a history of such an illness. Moreover, this was one ailment for which medical science had not found a cure. I was in disbelief. Here was a man who was physically fit, who did his daily yoga asanas, ate healthy food, went for daily walks and visited a doctor regularly. That such a thing could befall him seemed like a bad dream.

My semi-literate grandmother played down the issue. 'He's just stressed. All he needs is a little rest,' she said repeatedly.

I felt bad for my mother who already had her hands full—she had a husband who demanded her constant attention and a daughter who went everywhere but to school. Then there was me, who was flunking math. I vowed to help and go more often to Grandpa's house, as I still enjoyed his company. Sure, it meant listening to the same things over and over again. But it was fun in a way. He would speak about his college days in Lahore, his friends there, the house he grew up in and his neighbours—among whom he proudly included the Bollywood star Dev Anand.

My grandmother, however, refused to adjust. She fought with Grandpa and criticized him in the presence of others. There were numerous instances when Grandpa and I would be sitting together and she would walk in and say to me, 'Why don't you take him to a resort? Fresh air will cure his problem. All he does is sit here all day like a zombie.' Naturally, Grandpa got upset sometimes. He'd walk away silently into his bedroom while I protested and tried to reason with Granny. I requested her to deal with the problem placidly. After all, things could have been a lot worse: it could have been cancer or some kind of paralysis. We needed to remember the silver lining and thank the Lord.

A few weeks later, my mother received a telephone call. Something terrible had happened, she said. We rushed over to my grandparents' house in south Mumbai and found my grandmother sitting on the sofa and sobbing, holding her injured foot. Grandpa had attacked her, she said. Bouts of violence are common amongst Alzheimer's patients and this was our first experience with it. Something drastic had to be done. So we approached various old-age homes, but were turned down because they did not admit people with unsound mental health. Sadly, there was no institution in Mumbai that would care for a patient with this kind of illness.

After a lot of deliberation, my parents decided that Grandpa and Granny would have to move closer to us. We had rented out the first floor of our house, but now it was time for them to move into it. This would save us the trouble of travelling to south Mumbai from the suburbs every day, and monitoring and caring for them would become easier too.

But Granny didn't want to move. She had lived in her house for most of her life; she didn't want to leave her prized rose garden behind. To be fair the garden really was spectacular. It had the sweetest smelling roses one could ever find—yellow, white and, my personal favourite, red. Ever since I was a young boy, I had wanted to pluck a few and take them home. But alas, every time I tried to, I was caught and given an earful.

So we assured Granny that the garden would be tended to.

But then she brought up a new issue—the all-important 'kitty party', a gathering of women her age that she absolutely had to go to once a week. I volunteered to take care of Grandpa in her absence on those days. Finally, after a dozen more excuses, all of which were shot down, she agreed.

Within a few days, they had moved in with us. Nobody slept that first night after they arrived. Everyone stayed alert and kept their phones close.

When mother went downstairs with the morning tea the next day, she was greeted by a tired-looking Granny and a very chirpy Grandpa.

'Good heavens, you look terrible,' my mother said to Granny.

'That's because I haven't slept a wink,' came Granny's response. She had that look—the look a bull mastiff has when someone has taken its bone away. 'Your father kept me up all night. He was in the kitchen looking for food and dropped the utensils in the process. When I ran to see what had happened and protested, he threatened to slap me.'

'Oh my God,' said mother, her eyes and mouth open wide.

'Then he walked away and probably slept. Later, I woke up again when I felt something sitting on top of me,' Granny continued.

'Was it the cat?'

'No, it was your father. He mistook me for a cushion.'

Mother suddenly noticed yellow-stained clothes in the corner. 'What are those?' she asked.

'He has peed in his pyjamas and soaked them.'

Mother buried her face in her palms and then threw her hands up in the air helplessly.

Three more days went by in a similar fashion. On the fourth day, we saw some improvement with Grandpa sleeping soundly through the night.

Unfortunately, Granny had lost her patience by then. She packed her bags, ready to move back to her house in southern Mumbai. We tried convincing her but to no avail. She left anyway.

As the days went by, my involvement with Grandpa grew. I gave up cricket with friends in the evenings to take him out. We would hold hands and stroll around the building. It was sad that he was turning into a kid again, but we were both on the same page now. At the end of the walk, we routinely bit into our customary kulfis and smiled at each other.

Months later, there was another ill-fated incident. Granny was travelling to Khandala to visit her sister and my parents were out of town too. Since I had to look after Grandpa and his home, I decided to bring my stereo system and play him the only two Hemant Kumar songs that he remembered. When I entered the room, I found Grandpa in an animated conversation with the office boy who also helped out at home. The boy knew my grandfather's condition but after answering repeated questions about long-dead erstwhile business associates, he had reached his limit. The moment he saw me, he suggested that I grant him the rest of the day off. I thought about it and agreed. I was confident of handling Grandpa all by myself.

By the afternoon, the maid had completed the day's work and left. It was nearly half past three. I don't sleep in the afternoons, but Grandpa felt like taking a nap. He slowly walked to his bedroom, leaving me to my own devices.

Watching television would mean disturbing him, so I opted for reading the novel I had brought with me. The book was so dull that I was snoring within fifteen minutes.

Suddenly, Grandpa woke me up. 'Who are you?' he asked.

'I'm your grandson, Saurabh,' I responded, slightly rattled by the anger I saw on his face.

'Who's Saurabh?'

'Your grandson.'

'I don't have a grandson. Get out!' he hollered in rage.

'But I need to stay here and look after you.'

'I said get out.'

'No, calm down, Grandpa.'

He rolled up his sleeves and rushed at me, roaring, 'Don't make me do something I might regret later.'

'Please sit down!' I yelled at the top of my voice.

Taken aback at my unexpected reaction, he stumbled back to his bedroom, still muttering expletives.

I was in a dilemma. He wanted me to go, but I couldn't leave him alone to wander about and get lost outside or even run over while crossing the road. Frantically, I telephoned Granny, but her phone was unreachable. Soon, Grandpa walked into the room again and I froze with fear.

'Why haven't you left yet? I am the owner of this place. Get out!'

Before I could respond, 'Wham!' came the blow and I was knocked off my feet. He had missed my left eye by a whisker. Once again, he walked back to his bedroom and closed the door.

I sat on the sofa, nursing my injured cheek and thinking about the absurdity of what had just happened. Five minutes went by. The door opened and Grandpa came out with his hands behind his back. He saw me sitting there and walked slowly towards me with a stern look on his face. This time, I was prepared to duck or even run if required. There was no question of fighting back and hurting him of course.

Grandpa came and stood within a few inches of me, his hands still behind his back.

Then he extended his right hand and slowly caressed my cheek and wiped away my tears. And taking his left hand from behind his back, he presented me with a beautiful red rose.

The Dhaka Girl

by Dhrishti Dasgupta

The summer of 1947 was at an end and the mostly clear sky of Dhaka was painted with tints of orange and pink that afternoon. The wind roared through the date palms making them sway briskly, and it ran through the sand carrying away a part of it to destinations unknown. Dry leaves parted from the still young trees and flew with the wind to find their place in the blown-away sand while birds flocked over the dusty brown branches chirping merrily.

The rain was not too far. The scorching summer had prevailed a little longer that year, and now it was time to bid it adieu and hail the coming monsoon.

The thing about memories is that sometimes, you also remember the feelings attached to the moments from the past. I remember that that day, I felt as if the monsoon was going to bring a new beginning into our lives. I didn't know what it was going to be, but I just knew that whatever it was, it would be worth it.

The thick wooden stick rang out on the heavy iron gong, signalling the end of the school day, and the fourteen girls of our fourth-grade class got up, picked up their black slate boards and white slate pencils, and ran out of the broken-bricked school to the open land beneath the ample sky.

I rushed out too, for the wind was wonderful and untouched.

'Meera,' I heard someone call.

I turned, 'What?'

'It's going to rain, I guess,' Mouni said. 'Do you want to go to the nearby pukur and fish?'

'It would be awesome to have fish for dinner tonight,' I grinned.

'Woohoo!' Mouni exclaimed, and we hopped towards the large pond behind the school. By the time Mouni and I reached there, it had already started to rain. We took off our cotton stoles and threw them over the water, tying knots with the edges to make a sack-like structure. Then we moved the cloth slowly through the water, below the surface. It was a simple and efficient trap, but it demanded patience, and the vigorous movement of the fish, which the rain ensured.

After a long time, I noticed something in my trap. I pulled the cloth out of the water to find a smallish rohu fish trapped within. I jumped with excitement while Mouni made a face, since her luck was yet to turn.

More than an hour later, my stole had two fish while Mouni's had only one. But we were happy that we would be eating a delicious meal that evening. With my family of seven, it would be like sharing morsels, but still, even the thought of having that tiny share made me happy and content.

The afternoon was nearing its end; the direction of the sunrays behind the clouds told us that. We began our journey home, carrying the tiny bundle of fish in our arms. After walking together for a while, we parted and entered different streets.

Mouni and I were not only school friends but also family friends. Our fathers worked for the same British trading company as caretakers of the import–export goods. They earned a moderate amount of money that was just enough to feed their large families. The British companies were slowly withdrawing from the nation and we were just about scraping by on what we had. Buying fish for a meal was like an unfulfilled dream to us.

I skipped and hopped on my way while getting drenched in the rain; I kicked pebbles across the muddy street, waved to people I knew, and wondered how happy my mother and my four younger brothers would be to see the fish. I also knew that at dinner, my mother would tell us that eating fish upset her stomach, so that we, her five children, could each have a little more from her share. But I was not going to let her do that this time, because being a mother does not take away one's bucket of desires, it just buries them.

As I neared home, the excitement in me was palpable. I desperately wanted to see a glint of happiness in my family's eyes. I just couldn't wait.

When I was a street away from the house, my gaze fell on the huge banyan tree to my right. I saw a middle-aged man sitting beneath the tree with his knees drawn up to his chest and his arms wrapped around them. His head was bowed and his body was shivering continuously. He wore a pale blue salwar kameez that was marked by patches of dirt, and a white spherical cap on his head.

I paused for a moment and glanced at him. I realized that the man was sobbing softly. He looked worn out and his heartbreaking cry was pitiable. My heart sank every time he took a breath between sobs. The pain, the hurt, and the broken soul were clearly evident in his tears which were immediately washed away with the rain.

I could not hold myself back and, without realizing what I was doing, I walked towards him. At first, I was scared that he might turn out to be the kidnapper that my mother had warned me about but somewhere deep inside me, my soul didn't think that that painful cry was foul or fake. It was as true and pure as the love between the sky and the earth.

'Kaku, what happened?' I asked softly, reaching out to him.

He looked at me. His long beard was turning white with age. Wiping his tears with his forearm, he said, 'Nothing, Ma, nothing!'

'Then why are you crying?' I persisted.

He took a moment to catch his breath, and I looked straight into his eyes, innocently.

Taking out a few sets of glass bangles from his cotton bag, he said, 'I haven't been able to sell any of these for the past three days.'

He paused, and spoke again, 'The turbulence has started. We are not going to be one nation any more. Who will buy my bangles now when people are more concerned about saving their lives?'

I didn't understand what he was talking about that day. I just stood there, trying to figure out the reason behind his pain. I could only think of one—the unsold bangles.

'I have not made any money and my family hasn't eaten in days. This month of Ramadan has given us the strength to get through it,' he said, and a tear fell from his eyes. 'But tomorrow is Eid and I still don't have any food for them.'

'Tomorrow is Eid?' I asked sympathetically. He nodded his head in despair.

I thought for a while and said, 'If I wish to give you Eidi, will you accept it?'

He looked at me, surprised. He wondered what a girl of eight could possibly give him.

'Please?'

He nodded hesitantly.

I pulled out the bundle of fish from my arms and offered it to him.

'Two rohu fish. This is all I have.'

Tears welled up in his eyes as he accepted my Eidi with both hands. He could not stop sobbing. Those tears conveyed both his guilt at the inability to feed his family, and his happiness at the fact that his children wouldn't go hungry on Eid.

I felt happy. For the first time in my short life, I felt pleasure at giving something away.

'Sakina's favourite meal is fish and rice,' he said in a trembling voice. 'At least I'll be able to feed her fish tomorrow. Thank you so much.'

'Kaku, wait right here. I'll be back in a bit,' I said, and ran to my house.

It was a small one-roomed house with bare brick walls—incomplete and yet full of peace. To the right of the house stood a small berar ghor, a structure made out of bamboo poles and leaves for a makeshift refuge. That was our kitchen. I could see my brothers playing while my mother sat on the sandy porch peeling potatoes for dinner.

Shielded by the huge trees around, I crossed to the kitchen, staying out of sight. Unnoticed, I pushed the door open and went inside. I walked to the clay pot in the corner, removed its lid off and scooped out my share of rice for dinner on to a banana leaf. Then I folded the leaf and ran back to the banyan tree.

I smiled at the man and offered him the banana leaf along with its contents. He was astounded yet again, but this time he wasn't pleased.

'This is my share of rice,' I said. 'I know that this cannot help your entire family, but it should be enough for Sakina.'

'You have given me enough. I cannot take more from you,' he resisted.

'Please, Kaku, my Eidi would be incomplete without this.'

'Why don't you take these bangles from me in return?'

'If you gave me the bangles, then you would take away the pleasure of giving from me,' I said and smiled.

He took the rice and I happily walked back home.

At dinner, I pretended to have an upset stomach so that I wouldn't have to eat. Father started to worry about me, but my mother chose to ignore my symptoms since she suspected that I was responsible for the diminished amount of rice in the pot.

However, at night, I was so hungry that I could not fall asleep. Still, I continued to lie there, inert. Then, I overheard a conversation between my parents that stirred a realization in me—a new beginning was closer than I had thought.

'We must leave,' my father was saying. 'I don't know what lies ahead of us. We won't have this piece of shelter over our heads for long and we won't see this place ever again. I am afraid, what will I give you all there?'

'We can always choose to stay, can't we?' I heard my mother console him. 'This is our land and this is where we were born.'

'I don't think we have a choice. Our land is going to be taken from us.'

I may not have understood it all then but I knew that someday, we would have to go away forever. We would have to leave behind the beautiful hills that bore enchanting flowers, the melody of birds chirping over the trees, the sunshine that was so bright and comforting, the neatly plastered muddy porch where

I chased my brothers, and the smell of our land. Everything would stay, but only in our memories.

A couple of months later, I learnt that there were three kinds of people in the world: British, Hindu and Muslim. The British were the trespassers in our nation. Our nation was now freed of British rule, but the freedom had cost us dearly. Our nation was divided into two countries, India and Pakistan. The Hindus were meant to stay in India, while the Muslims belonged in Pakistan. Our Bengal, our land, was also divided. East Bengal would be a part of Pakistan.

My father had said that night that we had no choice but to leave. But he had been wrong. We had one more choice—to die in our motherland.

Riots had broken out. It was the end of humanity. It wasn't a war between religions. It was simply a war between one man who had lost all mercy and another who was helpless and wretched. Houses were burnt, girls were raped and people were killed inhumanly. Our Dhaka, our heaven, had turned into a battlefield of hell.

The Hindus who wanted to save their lives were running away to India, while most of those who didn't want to leave their motherland ended up losing their lives. We chose to try and escape.

My father planned our journey to West Bengal two days after the full moon day. For days, we shut ourselves in the house. We didn't even sit out on the porch any more. Hardly did we allow sunlight to intrude into the house, for we had nothing to do but wait for my father's friend who would help us board the train to India.

Our journey was to begin the next day. But destiny didn't give us enough time to cherish the last moments in our land. Early in the morning of the day before we were to leave, rioters broke into our neighbourhood. Somehow, we managed to run out before they could reach our home. We abandoned every single thing that we owned. I even left my only wooden doll behind.

We went and hid in the zamindar's mansion. The family was long gone. My father led us inside the zamindar's property and we went to the mango orchard at the back to hide. No one could spot us from a distance. But my father was restless. For the first time in my life, I saw fear on his face. He pretended to be strong on the outside, but on the inside, he was praying to God to give us one last chance to survive.

A few minutes later, my father stood up to leave for Mouni's house. He wanted to bring their family to the zamindar's mansion too. My mother didn't want him to leave but she knew that her husband was doing the right thing. Just as my father got up to leave, I stood up too. I insisted that he take me along with him, and he agreed reluctantly.

We crossed the streets like thieves, carefully measuring our steps. Soon, we reached Mouni's house. My father tightened his grip on my hand when he saw the house in front of us. Their berar ghor was now a heap of ashes. We didn't know whether Mouni's family was inside those ashes or if they had managed to escape. Even today, I don't know if Mouni is alive in some corner of this world or not. I would love to believe that she is.

When my father and I turned to go back, we saw someone looking at us. My father froze on seeing a Muslim man, but somehow he seemed familiar to me.

'Don't be afraid. I won't harm you. I am not inhuman,' the man said to my father politely. Then he looked at me, 'And you have been kind to me, Ma. How can I not return the favour?'

My father looked at me in surprise. I nodded in return.

'I will help you reach West Bengal. You can stay at my house until the time is right to leave,' the man said.

My father didn't seem to believe him.

'Trust me.' The man begged to be believed.

I looked at my father with my eyes filled with trust for the once-sobbing man. My father clutched my hand tighter and with tears in his eyes, he nodded at him.

Gathering the rest of our family, we reached Salim Chacha's house. That was his name. There, I met Sakina. She was a year younger than me and she was so beautiful. His house was too small to comfortably harbour twelve people at one time, but the warmth in the heart of Salim Chacha's family didn't make us feel unwanted at all.

That night, I learnt that are only two kinds of people in this world: human and inhuman, both independent of any religion.

The next morning, my mother and I wore burqas while my father and my brothers wore salwar kameezes and topis. Chacha thought that it was safer for us to travel this way. He came along with us and we took a bullock cart to reach the train station.

An hour later, we reached the spot where the train was supposed to halt. We stopped at a distance from the actual station. Getting down from the cart, I looked around and saw people everywhere. Everyone wanted to escape!

The train arrived and people boarded it like it was the only hope they had left from the sinking ship called life. We boarded the train too. I looked at Chacha and his eyes were so proud, as if he now had the courage to look straight into Allah's eyes and answer for all that he had done as a human. He looked at me and said, 'Meera, always remember— no religion is wrong and no soul is bad. It's just people who get misguided sometimes.'

The train whistled and a rush of agony went through our hearts, for we knew that we would never return to our land again. But we were happy that we were all alive and together.

Life is precious, even in the midst of a struggle. Those fearful days in the monsoon of 1947 introduced me to all the goodness of life even in its darkest hour. It silently said that once love is given in this universe, it can never go to waste; it will come back to you when you need it the most, in a form that you have never known.

*

'What happened after that?' I asked my grandmother when she stopped speaking.

'After that . . . life began.' Then she added, 'But that's a different story. Maybe some other time?'

'Yes, some other time.'

Agni Pareeksha

by Supriya Unni Nair

I first met Maneesha Ramakrishnan during Diwali in 2013. She was giggling like a schoolgirl at a random joke with her trademark twinkling eyes sparkling away. A mutual friend introduced us and told me that she was one of the survivors of the horrifying Carlton Towers fire of 2010. A short circuit had torched an office building, claiming nine lives and badly injuring seventy others. Maneesha had lost her voice in the accident and suffered damage to her internal organs. On top of it all, she was now in the middle of a legal battle with the building owners. But here she was in front of me, smiling and talking about the beautiful

Diwali lights, the riot of colours of the saris in the room, and the lovely cool Bangalore night.

Much later, when we became good friends, I asked her how someone who had gone through so much could be so devoid of bitterness. She gave me a huge smile and said simply, 'I choose not to be unhappy.'

*

The screams were getting louder and the acrid smell of burning rubber was getting stronger. The blanket of thick black smoke seemed to have taken on a life of its own, twisting and curling into macabre shapes. Maneesha crouched near the desk and watched the smoke inch towards her like a caped reaper. Was she imagining it, or could she really see the black skull and sunken hollow eyes, waiting to gather souls?

'Maneesha ma'am! Maneesha ma'am!' Fayaz the office boy's frantic cries jolted her back to reality. 'We have to get out!'

The smoke had blocked the stairway exit. They were seven floors up and the only way out was through the windows. Fear was making her nauseous and she could feel the bile rising in her throat.

Her thoughts raced to her two sons, 'My boys. My darling boys. I love you.' They were her life. Her everything. Raising them as a single mother had been tough, but it was the most gratifying experience of her life. She picked herself off the floor and looked around. People had collapsed. Her boss, Balaji, was vomiting and clutching his stomach. The efficient and strong Balaji—curled up like a child.

Across the room, the fire extinguisher lay in a corner. 'Who knows how to use a fire extinguisher?' thought Maneesha. Besides, it was useless against the raging might of the surging flames and smoke.

'Maybe we can break the windows,' she thought.

'Fayaz, help me with this,' she called out, her voice hoarse. Fayaz moved towards the extinguisher, coughing, his reed-like body shaking violently with each breath.

'How is he going to lift this? It's probably heavier than him,' thought Maneesha. She tried to take a deep breath, but the carbon monoxide scorched her lungs and sent her into a fit of coughing.

'I have to do this,' she told herself. She picked up the fire extinguisher with all her might and flung it against the window, cracking it in a bizarre zigzag pattern.

Down below, the rescue workers had spread a tarpaulin sheet and were encouraging people to jump.

Maneesha was sick with fear. Should she jump? Or should she wait till someone came up and rescued them? She felt nauseous and dizzy and sank down onto the floor, her lungs fighting against the carbon monoxide. Her throat felt like it was on fire. She began to pray, 'God, am I going to die? Are you watching?'

Maneesha heard the sound of footsteps and furniture being moved. The office was still dark. The smoke had diffused the narrow rays of light that were coming in from the crack in the window. She could catch parts of a conversation.

'There are people on the floor here!'

'We need to get them out!'

'I need more light. It's pitch dark!'

And then, 'Anyone here?'

Relief swept over her. Yes! Please help! She tried calling out but where was her voice? Perhaps screaming would help. She tried again but there was no sound—not even a whisper. She could hear the footsteps fading away.

'No! No!' Maneesha crawled towards where she

thought her desk used to be. 'Please wait!' she wanted to say.

Her body felt bloated. She dragged herself a little more but the footsteps were gone. 'This can't be happening,' she thought to herself. 'They will come back. They have to!'

She waited for what seemed like an eternity until another voice and another light came into the room.

'Anyone here?' He was so close to her that Maneesha could smell the dirt on his boots.

Yes! She cried out silently and then grabbed his trouser leg, shocking the rescue worker.

'Over here! I found someone!' He helped her up.

The descent down the seven floors was tortuous. Four people had to help her down the steps. One by one. Towards freedom. Towards life.

'Madam, you are smiling? Very good! Very good!' said the police officer who had come to help her. 'We will take you to hospital for a check-up first, okay?'

She smiled back, yearning to go home and be with the boys.

The hospital. The smells. The shocked look from the doctors and the wonderfully kind nurses. 'Why are they looking at me like that?' she thought.

Snippets of worried conversation floated in and out. 'Note the swelling . . .'

'She needs to be transferred to the ICU immediately.'

'We have to do a tracheotomy ASAP,' the doctor with the kind eyes said. 'This will help you breathe,' he explained to her.

But she just wanted to go home and wrap her boys in her arms.

The days seemed to melt into months. Two. Three.

Maneesha tried to make sense of everything. But there was so much pain—like a thousand daggers. There were tubes through her nose, her throat and her chest. She sensed bodies being carried out and heard anguished cries. She saw the concerned faces of her family. Her tough, Air Force pilot father looking down at her, his face etched with worry. Her strong and independent mother looking stunned. Then there were her babies—her firstborn Akarsh and her younger son Dhruv. Tears were streaming down their faces. 'Don't worry my darlings, we're going to get through this,' she wanted to tell them.

She drifted into a coma for three days.

Weeks later, she was the only Carlton Fire patient still in the hospital. The others had been discharged.

The kind sweet nurses labelled her the perfect patient. 'Maneesha loves us so much that she doesn't want to leave the hospital, isn't it?' a perky young nurse joked.

Eventually, they moved her out of the ICU. She had to learn how to breathe without the ventilator. More pain. More daggers. She had lost some forty kilos. 'Talk about instant weight loss!' she told herself.

There were more snippets of conversation. Someone was discussing money with her father. 'The government will bear the cost of the ICU,' she heard someone say.

'My purse,' Maneesha suddenly remembered. 'There was money in it . . . 25,000 rupees for Dhruv's fees.' She realized that the money must be ashes now, like the furniture and other 'important' documents at the office. 'Ashes to ashes, dust to dust,' thought Maneesha.

In the quiet of the night after everyone had left and she was with herself, she thought about her life. The struggles. Her failed marriage. Those frightening periods in her life when money was scarce. But on the positive side, her in-laws had loved her and had smothered her with affection. She had a great working relationship with her colleagues.

'I am so lucky to be alive. My body has fought for me,' she thought. 'God gives you two ropes to lasso life—a good one and a bad one. You have to choose. I choose the good rope. I'll live life to its fullest and I'll be happy.'

Eight months later Maneesha was finally discharged from the hospital. She was relieved to finally go home. But her vocal chords had been permanently damaged. She would always need the help of a tracheotomy tube to speak—it had been permanently inserted in her throat. Her kidneys had been affected and her lungs were damaged too. She looked at herself in the mirror—all skin and bones. Her hair had fallen out and her cheeks had sunk in. She was a ghost of her former self. Tears welled up in her eyes. 'What's the point? What do I do from here onwards?'

The image in the mirror seemed to answer her, like a whisper in the wind. *Nurture me. Nurture your two sons. Your parents and your friends. You even nurtured your ex-husband when he was almost dying. Now it's time to nurture me—your soul. Love yourself.*

'Yes,' Maneesha whispered back. 'Yes.'

It was an uphill task.

First, there was sustenance for the body. She had to

take care of her food and nutrition needs. There were boxes and boxes of medicines, innumerable check-ups and endless procedures.

Then, there was sustenance for the mind. She turned to books, to counselling, to friends and her boys. She watched the beautiful jacaranda trees bloom and enjoyed the lovely Bangalore weather. She spent time reading and laughing with her boys. She helped her friends, her house workers and the young flower girl who had problems at home. Her home became a sanctuary for wounded animals. 'I am a born nurturer,' she thought happily. 'That is my passion and calling in life—to nurture and to spread joy.'

And, there was litigation and more litigation. She had to go in and out of court seeking justice for herself and the other survivors.

And finally, she needed to get back to work. So she did. But the new multinational IT office with its efficient building made her feel suffocated. 'What am I doing here? I should be doing something I love. Life is too precious to waste,' she thought.

She quit and decided to follow her second passion— cooking. She catered for a friend's daughter's birthday party. Then another.

Then, one night, Maneesha was furious about the quality of the food her boys and she had ordered in. 'They charge so much and it tastes like this? I have half a mind to write to the owner and tell him that I can do a better job!' she fumed.

'Chill, Ma. If you're so upset, why don't you really write to him?' Akarsh said.

She did. After seven months, they responded, wanting to explore a possible collaboration.

But the biggest demon was yet to be slayed. Maneesha had to go back to Carlton Towers. She had tried and failed. Her legs had turned into jelly at the sight of the soot marks on the walls. The news that some of her beloved colleagues had jumped to their deaths had crushed her. The demons tormented her. Surely there was a place beyond the fear of Carlton Towers. But how would she find it?

'Dhruv, will you organize a flash mob for me?' Maneesha asked her younger son one day.

He was amused at her question, 'Sure Ma, but with whom?'

'With me and your friends . . . at the Carlton,' answered Maneesha.

The boy was silent for a while. Then he looked at her and smiled. 'Yes, of course. Let's do it.'

On 23 February 2013, three years to the day after the Carlton fire, Maneesha, Dhruv and his friends, and other family members of the tragedy celebrated Beyond Carlton. They danced. They lit paper lanterns with the names of the deceased and released them into the air.

Finally, Maneesha felt at peace. She had slayed her demon.

*

In the *Ramayana*, the 'agni pareeksha' or trial by fire was something Sita was asked to undergo to prove her chastity. The fire rewarded her virtue by leaving her unscathed. Maneesha Ramakrishnan's trial by fire was just as harsh. And she was rewarded with life. She says the secret to her positivity lies in the simplest of things: gratitude for each and every simple pleasure of life.

Elixir

by Satyarth Nayak

My mother was packing my bags when my phone started to ring. *Her* name flashed on the screen. But what was flashing before my eyes was the sour fight we had had two days ago. I disconnected.

'What if he pees all over me?' I asked my mother to distract myself.

Her left eyebrow leapt in the air.

'Your bladder wasn't so high and dry when you were a baby on his lap. Think of it as payback.'

We both made faces and laughed. She knew I was joking. She knew how much I loved my grandfather and how thrilled I was that a few hours later, I would be sitting next to him once more. She also knew how distressed I was that his good health was slowly leaving him, like so many of his old friends.

Hobbling towards the ninetieth year of his life, my grandfather had enjoyed a remarkably healthy constitution for eighty-five years. But the last five years had suddenly turned dark. The fading light had made him a distant person who did not speak much. He knew who we were, and still, sometimes, his eyes stared at us like the plastic ones on my sister's fluffy bear. He would often lie down and shudder as pain racked his body. And now, out of the blue, I was told that he had started wetting the bed too.

'How's Grandma taking it?' I queried.

'She's living with it.'

'Living? The woman must be livid. It's a wonder she hasn't hacked off his pee-pee by now.'

'Zip it.' Mother glared at me as she delivered a plate of food into my hands. 'She loves that man. I have never understood why you find that so hard to believe.'

I chewed in silence. What was there to believe? Of course they had been man and wife for some sixty years now but I had never been witness to anything remotely like love between the two of them. I also knew the story of their marriage, which had further convinced me that there was nothing fairy-tale about their alliance. Grandma was the eldest daughter of a big zamindar while Grandpa was the only child of a farmer couple. It sounded like a classical recipe for a love story but that's not what happened. Our hero had risen from the soil and cracked a top government job in the tax department that had led the girl's father to fix their nuptials. That was the end of the story—just a feudal woman and a proletariat man yoked together in an arranged marriage, exchanging vows at the altar of social mobility.

Though Grandpa had triumphed in climbing several rungs of the social ladder, Grandma never missed an opportunity of reminding him of his rustic ancestry that reeked of cow dung and pesticides. He, on the other hand, would look at me with a crooked smile each time Grandma imported an English word into her vernacular sentences. She would moan about how her father had 'sabotaged' her life by marrying her off to a country bumpkin who spent his days drawing geometrical maps of the village lands. He would drone on about how she wasted her time reading Hindi pulp fiction for cheap thrills. She loved to hate how Grandpa had a gooey heart for his extended clan, and he loved to hate how Grandma glued herself to the phone and bitched for hours about everyone. It was a miracle, I often thought, that despite such despicable sentiments for each other, they managed to produce not one or two but four offspring. For all we knew, I mused, the task might have been accomplished while she was turning the page of another wretched thriller and he was drawing the hypotenuse on another sorry map.

'With Grandpa's present condition, I am surely going to find her a lot more militant,' I said to no one in particular.

Mother shook her head but I knew what I was saying. The last five years had turned dark for my grandmother too but in a much more literal way. Glaucoma had silently sneaked inside both her eyes and smashed out the bulbs. I was witness to her running from doctor to doctor begging each one for a glimmer of vision, but it had not happened. Her soul had begun to rot after that. Self-pity, rage and despair can elbow out all the love from a person's heart and in this case, there had not been very much for Grandma to begin with.

But Mother was still shaking her head, 'I know what they mean to each other. You'll see.'

I had seen enough, I thought—seen that my grandparents were wonderful human beings by themselves, but put them together in a beaker and you had a 'chemical locha'. That's how most relationships were, weren't they? When a sixty-year-old relationship could inspire no love in my grandparents' hearts, my paltry six-month-long affair burdened with friction was going to be nothing more than an empty glass of water.

She was calling again. I disconnected. Romantic love was a chimera after all.

Standing before my grandmother nine hours later, I could see her empty eyes trying to imagine how I looked since she had seen me last. It was as if her face was grabbing at my voice and using it to sketch a picture of me. Her despair seemed to have made space for acceptance. But the self-pity was intact, and so was the fury.

'No one comes to me now. Not even death. So many people are dying, but not me. I know I will keep living and suffering. This blind life is not going to leave me so soon.'

'Where is Grandpa?'

'He must be lying around somewhere. All he does is sleep and piss. Piss and sleep. And he doesn't even drink water. I wonder what more I have to suffer before the end. Hell is right here in my house.'

'We should get him checked again.'

'I keep saying that but no one has the time. I have told everyone now that they must either take the old man to the doctor or put him on the funeral pyre. I don't care.'

I walked across the dining hall and entered the small room that was Grandpa's refuge. He was lying flat on the spring bed, but he wasn't asleep. He grinned at me as I rested my head on his chest. We both knew what was coming. One of the million things he had taught me as a child was an old Oriya lyric with words so haunting that they had engraved themselves in my memory. I loved nothing better than hearing the words in his cracking voice.

He sat up. It was time for an encore.

'Raha raha khyane baaspiya sakata
Dekhibi Chilika chaaru chitrapata.'

The son of the soil begging the steam engine to chug slowly, slowly—so that he could stare a little longer at the beauty of his beloved land that had inspired him. It was the cry of a departing soul who was pleading. Pleading for a moment more . . . just a moment more.

Then the mood suddenly shrivelled and died. The raucous tune of a recent Bollywood duet blew in from Grandma's room and invaded the moment. I turned and saw Grandpa's face change.

At dinner, they did not speak. Their conversations had always been lone-word exchanges but even those seem to have been abandoned now. And funnily enough, it had ceased to be awkward. Grandma got up, fumbled for the walls and walked into her room holding on to them as Grandpa watched silently.

Whenever I was in Orissa, I always slept with my grandparents. It was a vestigial remnant of my childhood days, and the three of us had still not grown out of it. Even when I used to hit the sack with one of my cousins, I would wake up in the middle of the night to find Grandpa dragging me back to their bed. Tonight was no exception. I soon fell asleep lulled by the familiar melody of their nasal snoring.

I dreamt that I was floating. Floating on a river.

Alone on a cold, cold river. It was getting colder and colder and the river seemed to get wider and wider. I opened my eyes. This was no river. Grandpa had wet the bed.

Tearing through the mosquito net, I yanked at the light switch and saw what I had been hearing about all these months. His pyjamas and legs were reeking of urine. The liquid was slowly spreading over the blue bedsheet like a dark cloud, but what was turning me cold was the way his fragile body was reacting to the mishap. He was trembling like a plucked guitar string as if embarrassed at his juvenile deed. Half-awake now, the man was moaning like a dog out on a winter night. He was thrashing his legs to get the urine off his skin but the sticky liquid clung to his pores like so many leeches. I turned to dash out of the room and get my uncle when a different sound stopped me.

Grandma was awake.

She was talking. Talking to my grandfather. She was not screaming. She was soothing him. Soothing her ninety-year-old husband as if he was her nine-year-old son. Speaking to him in a voice I had never heard before.

And then something happened.

I saw Grandpa stretch his hand across the bed towards her . . . slowly. I gulped. If only Grandma could see and reach out to him . . .

But I was wrong. She turned. Turned towards him and extended her hand. She knew. She somehow knew. She was groping. Groping along the wet surface. Groping for him until their fingertips touched. I saw her take his shivering hand and squeeze it in her palm. Tighter and tighter. The more he convulsed, the tighter she clenched. The spasms rocked him again and again but she held on tightly, not once letting go of those withered fingers.

They were silent now. Only their pulses throbbed together. Moments later, Grandpa's hand relaxed. His frame stopped trembling, and gradually he fell asleep. Grandma opened her fist. As she gently pulled her hand away, I saw a single tear slide down her cheek and smudge the pillow.

The next morning, she yelled at me to hike the volume of her tape recorder and he walked out of the room grinding his false teeth. But I was smiling. Smiling because while walking out, Grandpa had drawn the curtains to keep the sun out of Grandma's face—and she was calling out to me again asking what I was doing for Grandpa's birthday next week.

I knew something now. Love is like all those nice things around us that aren't always visible. Like a rainbow. You don't always see it. You just have to trust that it's there.

I took out my cell phone and dialled her number.

The Right to Refuse

by Jimmy Mathew

The people of the town considered it to be a city. But I was not impressed. Nobody there seemed to know what a reconstructive plastic surgeon really did. Fortunately, the orthopaedist was convinced of my utility with the number of trauma cases that came in. And I needed the job. The most boring part, however, was the Out Patient Department visits.

My hopes soared as a young couple walked in. The girl was pleasantly plump and pretty in a droopy way. Did she require liposuction? A nose job, perhaps? I glanced towards the man with her; he seemed to be the sullen, high-testosterone types. The front of his scalp was a sparse wasteland. Maybe it was the man who wanted a hair transplant?

No, something was wrong. The girl was weepy and the man looked furious.

He gruffly introduced himself and his wife. They were married just a few days ago. He said, 'Doctor, she was not a virgin. I could tell on the first night. I am not a fool. I know these things.' The words had a malignant finality to them.

'No, I swear on God . . .' The girl blurted out. Then she lowered her head and wept.

Hesitantly, I started telling them about how the hymen can be very delicate in some women and how exercise or stretching could have played a part in tearing it. Or it may have been, well . . . not noticeably tough. I paused doubtfully.

The man was dismissive, 'I have no doubt. But I am willing to forgive her.' He made a magnanimous gesture with his hand. 'I want you to restore her hymen. You have to do an operation on her.'

'What?' I couldn't help exclaiming. My stiff upper lip, the mark of a decent medical man, had gone to pieces. I put things together in my mind with some difficulty.

I carefully weighed my words before I spoke again, 'Virginity is an idea. I have no objection to you giving such inflated importance to it. The fact that she told you she did not lose it before marriage should be enough. How can an artificially made hymen make up for it?'

'I just want to have that satisfaction,' the man said with the hideous semblance of a smile.

'You won't get it. At least not through my hands,' I said.

'What do you mean?'

'I won't do it. That's all. You are free to consult anybody else,' I was firm.

His eyes bulged and his face took on an incensed reddish hue. I stared back calmly, mentally preparing for an imminent physical attack.

He stormed out along with the girl. I followed them out and saw Sugunan, the young OPD nursing assistant, staring at their retreating backs. 'I know her,' he said absentmindedly. 'She is Nandini, my neighbour. She is a nice girl. I had attended the wedding.' He had enough sense not to ask what they had come for.

The next day, I was surprised to see her waiting alone in the OPD. Her eyes were swollen and puffy.

'Please perform the surgery, doctor,' she begged. 'Otherwise, my life will be ruined.'

This was agony. It was one of those hard situations where I felt sorry for her and yet, I couldn't bring myself to perform a surgery I didn't believe in. I felt as if I was being put through the wringer.

She was crying as she walked out of my room. I had refused her request for a hymenoplasty.

Sugunan was standing outside the door and was shocked to see her crying. I saw Nandini give him a weak smile through her tears. He looked at me enquiringly.

'Is she a friend?' I asked.

He nodded.

'She's in a little trouble. Why don't you go and talk to her?' I said on an impulse.

Sugunan ran after her.

I called for my next patient. It was a couple. The man looked studious and portly and the young woman was dark and attractive. The swollen eyelids and general demeanour denoted recent crying.

'Here we go again,' I thought.

I was usually inundated with weepy young women. Just like other men afflicted with masculinity, tears from women made me especially uncomfortable. I had an irresistible urge to run to the next district whenever I saw a woman crying. But I guess they were as unavoidable as taxes, tables and tiresome males. I felt a sudden surge of anger at all the men who made women cry. 'It isn't fair,' I thought. 'Why can't men realize that women are beautiful and delicate beings who need tender handling? Why can't women be treated with extreme gentleness and care?' I conveniently forgot my own transgressions that had sent scores of women associated with me to weep and cry with unrestrained abandon at various periods of my life.

I fixed the man with a baleful eye, 'What's the matter? How can I help you?'

The man cleared his throat, 'Er . . . her nose is not right. She wants a bigger nose.'

I looked at her small straight nose. One could not imagine a more perfect nose. In fact, one could not imagine a more perfect face.

'I think the nose is perfect. It is very difficult to improve upon this. What exactly is the problem with it?' I enquired cautiously. I was always very guarded with rhinoplasties. One had to be, especially when the complaints were vague and the deformity small or non-existent. Besides, it was an urban legend among our professional community that dissatisfied nose-job patients had murdered seven cosmetic surgeons till date. I didn't want to be the eighth.

'Okay, leave it. Can you do anything about the chin? Make it longer, for instance. Do you think you could make it small?' the man said in a rush.

I stared at him.

He quickly corrected himself, 'Smaller, I mean. Don't you think that a smaller chin will give more balance to her face?'

I am afraid I sort of lost my temper at that point. 'Are you the one who wants all these surgeries? Why doesn't she speak? Did you force her to come to me? For what?' I almost shouted.

'No, doctor. I want the surgery,' the girl spoke up for the first time.

'What is it that you want exactly?'

'My face is all wrong.' she replied.

'I have to know exactly what is bothering you about your face. Otherwise, I can't help you.'

'My eyes, eyebrows, nose and chin—everything is wrong. I don't like the length of my face either. I want a more moon-like face. The nose and chin also have to be changed.' She sounded desperate.

There were some psychiatric conditions like this. But why was the young man colluding with her? Suddenly, the truth struck me and I questioned the girl, 'You don't want people to recognize you! That's why you want to change your appearance. May I ask why?'

It was clear from their faces that they had been caught. I was soon rewarded with a remarkable story.

Mary had an ailing father and a brother who had to be enrolled in college. She turned to prostitution as a way out and got many high-paying clients over a period of one year. That was when Sunil came to her too. It was his first time. Sunil fell in love with her and wanted to marry her. But he was a driver and many of Sunil's friends and fellow townsmen knew about Mary. She was trapped in her shady reputation.

The girl was ready to make any sacrifice to marry Sunil. He loved her too, but how would he handle the humiliation of marrying a prostitute? That was the gist of the couple's dilemma. And they thought that I was the perfect solution.

'I can't help you with the surgery. But let me see what else I can do,' I said.

I took out my cell phone and dialled Sandeep's number. He was one of my closest friends and a classmate from medical school. Now, he had a chain of clinics across Dubai and Abu Dhabi.

After a short chit-chat, I asked Sandeep if he needed a driver for one of his ambulances.

One year later, when I went to visit Sandeep in Dubai, I was invited as an honoured guest to Sunil and Mary's house. The couple had a small but neat apartment. A one-month-old baby lay in the crib with her rosy eyelids tightly shut. She was smiling in her sleep.

'That was quick work,' I winked at Sunil.

'The way you solved our problem was also quick,' he said. 'I have a surprise for you—somebody is coming to meet you right now.'

The doorbell rang and Sugunan, my erstwhile nursing assistant, walked in. He had left India to come to Dubai six months ago and had taken a recommendation letter from me to Sandeep for possible employment. So I was not surprised to see him. But I was really surprised to see Nandini standing by his side. He had an arm around her. I remembered Nandini well because of her odd request.

'We ran away,' Sugunan explained. 'She has filed for a divorce.'

On the way back from Sunil's home, I reflected on the strange ways of the world. I thought about virgins and former prostitutes and then about men and their different attitudes. Then I thought about coincidences—or were they simply the mysterious ways of providence?

The day I went back to the hospital, the hospital administrator Puneeth came to meet me. 'We know that you are good, doctor. But your conversion rate isn't that great,' he said.

'Conversion rate' is a term used in hospital finance. It denotes the percentage of patient consultations that get converted to revenue-generating procedures such as surgeries.

I replied, 'A liposuction—fifty thousand rupees for the hospital.'

He looked at me enquiringly.

'A rhinoplasty—sixty thousand rupees.'

I paused for effect as he stared at me.

'The right to refuse a wrong procedure—priceless.'

Father's Reading Glasses

by Vibha Lohani

Father, like almost every other fifty-something government employee, had two pairs of glasses—one for reading and another for distance vision. That was the trend in the eighties, when people didn't really have any other choice.

My family considered my teen rebellious phase to be a problem, but Father's glasses were an even bigger problem, because he kept losing them more often than I lost my temper. And guess whose job it was to look for them—mine, of course!

I was the youngest in our family of five— Grandmother, Father, Mother, an elder sister and me. Everybody seemed to have something against me. Grandmother thought I was too wild for a girl; Mother thought I was too argumentative; and as for my sister, that I was her sibling was problem enough. I, on the other hand, thought that I was simply unlucky enough to be stuck with the wrong family. The only person who did not seem to have a problem with me was Father. So I really had no reason for not doing whatever he asked of me, even if it was repeatedly looking for his reading glasses.

Father claimed that I was the only expert who could find his glasses, and I was secretly proud of my skill.

One morning during the summer vacations, my sister and I had a big fight over whose bed should be near the window. We often rearranged our room and it was filled with posters of film stars and funky quotes. On hearing our shouts, Mother came into our room and started scolding us. Suddenly, Father called, 'Vibha, I can't find my reading glasses. Come here and help me find them.'

Mother paused for a moment and said, 'Go look for Father's glasses first or else he will be late for office.'

I exited the room and ran down the staircase

muttering to no one in particular, 'When anyone has work, I have to do it—but when I want something, I am always asked to compromise. Just because Sister has her board exams, I am supposed to adjust with her on everything. What has sleeping by the window got to do with exams?'

By the time I had finished grumbling, I was already standing before Father. He looked up from the newspaper and said, 'I can't find my glasses.'

I looked at him and despite my anger, smiled and said, 'They are resting on your nose, Pa.'

'These are my long-distance glasses. I don't know where I've kept the reading ones,' said Father.

I was very fond of reading detective stories and in typical Agatha Christie style, I enquired, 'Where did you last see the glasses and what were you doing at the time?'

Father thought for a while and replied, 'I was cleaning both the pairs in the veranda.'

I made a wry expression with narrowed eyes and a twisted mouth (it was my assumption that detectives thought with such expressions while solving crimes) and then announced, 'You must have kept the reading glasses on the dashboard of the car instead of the long-distance ones! Give me the car keys and I will get them for you.'

Father obediently handed me the keys and I procured the glasses from the very place I had said they would be in. Bingo! Father patted my back and said, 'I don't know how you were able to find them. I am sure I looked for them there before I called you.'

I smiled.

Mother was in the kitchen, so I quietly rushed back to my room to finish the war with my sister. But she seemed to have lost interest in continuing the fight. Now, the two beds were by the wall and the study table was by the window with thick curtains drawn across it.

Days went by and each and every mission to look for Father's glasses became more extensive. Sometimes I found them in Grandmother's medicine drawer where he had left them after checking the expiry date on the medicines; sometimes they were in the newspaper rack, sometimes near the washbasin, sometimes on top of the refrigerator and sometimes even inside it.

Now, my father was a very organized man and quite particular about keeping things in place. But his reading glasses seemed to be the exception. He lost them so often that one day, Mother fixed a string to their temple bends so that Father could hang the pair around his neck. This arrangement lasted for around a week or ten days, after which the string broke from Father's constant pulling and fiddling, and he managed to lose his glasses again that same evening.

Time passed and on a random Sunday, Mother asked me to finish my homework before the evening because some guests were coming and she would need help later. Since my sister was in college by then and staying in a different city, I was the default help around the house.

But I was also a book addict. I had borrowed a Poirot novel that I hadn't read yet from the school library—it had to be returned the very next day. So reading won over homework and the moment Mother called for help, I yelled back, 'Mother, I am doing my homework!'

She came and started scolding me and immediately, I started arguing about how I was being treated like a slave in the house. This was just about to be the concluding scene of my Sunday when Father called out, 'Vibha, I can't find my reading glasses. Come here and help me find them.'

Before Mother could say anything further, I rushed to him like an obedient daughter. My father needed me and I needed to save myself from Mother's scolding.

Once again, I started my enquiry session with him, 'Where were you before this, Pa? When did you last use the glasses?'

Finally, I found his glasses in the puja room, comfortably resting near Ganapatiji's feet.

Sometimes, I wondered if the glasses had magical feet that they walked away to all these strange places. But I was sure of one thing—I was the only one who could find them. It never struck me that I was the only one who was asked to find them.

Two years whizzed past and it was my turn to go to a college hostel in another city. I was very excited and looked forward to the days ahead. My only worry was how Father would find his reading glasses now without my help.

By the time I completed my graduation, Father too was transferred to the same city. Grandmother had passed away by then and my sister was married, so only Mother and Father had to relocate. They were happy to have at least one child living with them and I was happy to have the comforts of home again.

It was enjoyable in the beginning and then it became a way of life. There were small arguments with Mother, she constantly complained about me being a fussy eater, and then there was Father, who still kept losing his glasses! Now, finding his glasses was much more urgent, since he had only a single pair of glasses with bifocal lenses for both reading and distance vision.

So I was back to my old job of hunting for Father's glasses.

Mother was a teacher and she too had been using reading glasses for a very long time, but she never lost them. The only time I remember Mother's glasses being misplaced was when Father thought that they were his glasses and wore them for a while before losing them somewhere.

I had grown up from being a rebellious teenager to a working adult—I actually had a job post my MBA. Life had become so busy that sometimes I came home just to eat dinner and sleep. There was hardly any time to myself and when there was, I spent most of it sleeping. Mother and Father tried to explain the necessity of rest but when you are in your early twenties, you feel that you can conquer the world. Soon, the stress started taking a toll on my health.

It was like being a teenager again. I was always grumpy and irritable. My temper flared up at the slightest provocation and sometimes, without any at all. I managed to keep a straight face in the office but not for long. The stress became so evident on my face that Mother and Father started to worry. Still, I was not ready to stop or re-evaluate my lifestyle.

One day, I was unnecessarily arguing with Mother over something I don't even remember now when I heard Father call out the same words after a long time, 'Vibha, I can't find my reading glasses, come here and help me find them.'

I smiled. I had understood the meaning of that call by now. Anger Management may sound like a big corporate phrase, but Father had healed me with a simple therapy—when my fuse threatened to blow, I just had to search for his reading glasses.

Aagneya

by Rajesh Pooppotte

It was a pleasant Friday evening. When her father returned from office and did not see her in the hall, he asked, 'Where is Aagi?'

No one spoke. There was only silence. Her mother's face said it all—something serious had happened.

Worried, he ran about the house and finally found his daughter sitting in a corner of the bedroom. It was clear from the marks on her face that she had been beaten. The moment she saw her father, Aagi's eyes filled with tears. He felt something break in his heart. He hugged her close to his chest. He kissed her forehead. It seemed to make her feel better.

He was furious at his wife's behaviour.

He told Aagi that he would be back and went to speak to his wife. 'What the hell is this?' he demanded. 'How could you . . .?'

Again, there was a stubborn silence. This was usual at their home. His wife never told him what was going on. But he would not give up this time. He had to break the silence.

He strode to the kitchen, picked up a steel plate and dropped it deliberately on the floor. The plate bounced and hit the wall with a loud steely noise.

Immediately, his wife responded angrily. 'Do you know what your darling daughter has done? She hit a boy in her class and it almost took out his eye. He is in hospital now. Luckily, he is not in any danger. What if there was some permanent damage? She would have been expelled from school!'

As a father, he could not believe it. He knew that Aagi was a little naughty—but she could not purposely hurt someone, could she?

Aagneya—that was her name. But everyone called her Aagi. She had been born to them after years of trying, and a lot of prayers. She had grown up being showered with love by the people around her. The eight-year-old girl had already captured everyone's heart with her words and thoughts. She was funny and expressive whenever she narrated the incidents at school. She had many friends, ranging from children to old people. She was like the sun that shines through the clouds, like the breeze that blows after the first shower of the rainy season. She was his darling Aagi! Words could never do her justice. You had to meet and talk to her to really know her. Her father thought about how cute she looked in her pink dress and couldn't resist a smile. She was everyone's favourite, but she was her daddy's daughter. He was more of a friend to her than a parent.

No, her father concluded, he was sure that she was not at fault. He tried to calm down. The boy and his family must be undergoing pain too, he thought. Whatever the reason, Aagi should not have hurt him so badly. His mind kept searching for an explanation. Finally, he decided to talk to her and give her some advice.

Slowly, he sat down next to her and patted her head gently, 'Dear, what happened? Why did you hurt that boy?'

Sobbing, she replied, 'Daddy, he pulled my dress.'

'So you hit him?'

She took some time to reply, 'I was playing and this boy suddenly came and pulled at my dress. I tried to push him away. I had a pencil in my hand and the pointy end hit him hard on his eyebrow.'

Though she was crying, her explanation seemed reasonable. The incident sounded very normal—like an accident that can happen between two kids. However, little Aagi did not say that she was sorry about it and her father wondered why.

He took her to the small park near their house and they sat down on an iron bench. Many children were playing near them. They did not speak for a long time. Aagi's tears had dried and the tearstains marked her cheeks. Her hair was a mess and hadn't been combed since the morning. He was concerned and worried about how he would broach the topic with her. He didn't want her to feel that he did not support her. So he simply continued to sit with her in silence. The leaves on the trees were not moving either, almost as if they all wanted to listen to what she had to say.

After a long time, he took her cold palm in his hand. She closed her eyes and leaned against him. She felt safe. Her silence made him worry more, though.

Finally, he asked her, 'Do you want to go and play with the other children?'

There was a long pause. Then, she shook her head.

'Darling, these things will happen when you play with your friends. But why did you push and hit the boy? You should have gone and told your teacher. What if you had poked him right in the eye? You wouldn't have been able to go to school after that. Do you know that? Do you have any idea about how much pain he must be going through now?'

Her head was bowed, but he was sure that she was listening. And yet, there was no response.

'Had it been more serious, the police might have come and taken you to jail,' he continued, trying to get a reaction out of her.

Now, she suddenly looked up at him, but there was no fear in her eyes. He realized that even an eight-year-old girl these days understood what might send a person to jail, and what might not.

She spoke in a low voice, 'Okay, Daddy. Now I want to tell you something.'

He was waiting for this moment—waiting for her to speak her mind.

She asked him, 'Have you seen *Mahabharata* on TV?'

He was confused at the change of subject. He almost lost his temper. With difficulty, he controlled himself and nodded. 'Yes, of course,' he said.

'When Dushasana Uncle pulled Draupadi Aunty's sari, she cried for help. But nobody came forward to help her. It was Lord Krishna who heard her cry and helped her. Later, in the Kurukshetra war, Bhima Uncle pulled out Dushasana Uncle's arms for touching Draupadi Aunty, tore open his chest and killed him. He then took Dushasana Uncle's blood and poured it on Draupadi Aunty's head to keep his promise of revenge.

'Today, there was no one to help me so I just tried to protect myself. When that boy pulled my dress, my underwear was showing. Everyone in the classroom was looking at me and some were even laughing. This boy had done the same thing earlier to my classmate Roshni too. Why should I allow him to insult me? If I allow him to pull my dress today, he will tear someone else's tomorrow. I didn't want to hurt him, but at the same time, I didn't want to get hurt either. When I defended myself, I had a pencil in my hand—and it simply hit him on the eyebrow. I feel bad for him, Daddy, but it was not my mistake. He started it all. Did I really do something wrong?'

He noticed the spark in her eyes and did not know how to respond. Her reply had made him think. Should he feel proud about what she had done?

He searched for some faulty logic in what she had said, but could find none. She had taught him an important lesson of self-respect. Her example from the *Mahabharata* rang true, at least for him. One of the main reasons for the Kurukshetra war was the humiliation of Draupadi. And the punishment for abuse in those days was a horrible death. These days, one saw and heard about so many incidents of abuse. No matter what their age, women were being abused in different ways—right from the time they were in their mother's womb till the time they went to their graves. Were all the culprits being punished? Were the victims getting justice?

We live in the same country, he thought, where legends fought, killed and died for the sake of dharma. It was said that when dharma failed, there would be a new generation of heroes who would be born to bring it back. Draupadi was born to King Drupad after years of prayer. She was born from fire. Aagneya too was born after a long wait and much effort. The meaning of her name was 'daughter of fire'. Maybe there were some similarities between the two of them after all.

The new generation of girls have Draupadi in their blood, he thought. People who thought of harming them would end up in big trouble. If all the little Draupadis started to respond to every threat and act for their protection, then all the evil men and women would soon have to find a place to hide. What happened to the boy was unfortunate, but surely he would always think twice before he touched any girl's dress ever again, even playfully.

He pulled his daughter to his chest.

A New Beginning

by Swaha Bhattacharya

In another world, we might have been soulmates. In this one, we liked getting in each other's way, treading on each other's toes, creating potentially dangerous situations, signing a reluctant truce and then starting all over again. We were sisters. Actually, we were cousins—but since we had grown up in the same home, it felt like we were sisters. We were also friends, covering for each other when it was needed, though we really couldn't stand each other most of the time.

While Didi was more the outgoing kind, I preferred to keep to myself. While she sparkled in the sun, I revelled in the soft darkness I had created around me.

I took everything way too seriously. She navigated through every mess like nothing could stop her, nothing at all. Her perkiness and exuberance made my frequent rainy days seem cloudier than usual; her acting like every day was a big roaring party got on my nerves a little too often.

We were nineties' kids, instinctively trying to hold on to the remaining shreds of a world that was fast slipping away. We went through the Calcutta monsoons together—wading through the Lake Market alleys and learning to find our bearings around the city. We bickered all the time but for reasons that were purely selfish, we tolerated each other. Didi used me as an excuse to stay out late, and she became my alibi whenever I wanted to give my parents the slip. She introduced me to my first nightclub experience at Tantra, bought me my first and only pair of Jimmy Choos, and sat through every tragic experiment on my tresses and every painful tattoo session.

We weren't special. We were just two girls growing up in the city tentatively treading through childhood and adolescence. If someone ever told me then that the girl alongside me—the girl with the wavy hair with nerdy glasses and braces on her teeth—would have a story that was extraordinary, I would have scoffed a little and laughed.

During the day, Didi was perpetually being shouted at by someone or the other for lazing around or bunking classes. By night, she became the official agony aunt flooded with distress calls from friends that lasted into the wee hours. Often, I'd wake up in the middle of the night hearing the phone ring, and Didi would whisper into the receiver to avoid waking me. 'I see,' she'd say, 'well, you can try something different. No, I don't think taking your life is a good idea . . . no, no, not at this moment.'

We were a family of eight living in a house on Manohar Pukur Road. As is common with most joint families, Didi and I were raised jointly by our mothers. In fact, she often came to my mother seeking permission for things she knew her own mother would not agree to. My mother always took Didi's side in nearly every argument. I guess it was with this faith that Didi broke the news to my mother. The decision proved to be a poor one. All hell broke loose instantly.

It all started with a casual visit. On a Sunday, Didi decided to call on one of her oldest friends,

Preeti. I tagged along with the hope of catching the latest Bollywood flick in Priya cinema on the way back. When we reached Preeti's house, she appeared quite glum. The reason was her neighbour, she said. Didi had just opened her mouth to make a caustic comment about neighbourly feelings when she was cut short by a shadow that fell across the door.

The little girl peeped at us, shy and afraid to come out from behind the door. Preeti playfully scooped her up into her arms. 'This little doll is Diya,' she said. 'She lives next door with her daddy!'

Six-year-old Diya clapped her hands and gave us the most heartbreakingly beautiful smile. She was a cherubic angel with a mass of curly waves on her head and dimpled cheeks.

But I wasn't looking at her. My attention was caught by the expression on Didi's face. I had never seen that look before and I didn't know what it meant, except that my sister had never looked so pristinely beautiful until that moment—it was as though she had found the fount of all happiness.

We heard Diya's story from Preeti. Diya and her father had been Preeti's neighbours for some years. The girl's mother had passed away in childbirth and they had no other family to speak of. They did not have much—just enough to live on—but they were happy. Diya had started school a year ago. A few months ago, her father had been diagnosed with a terminal disease. It was in the final stages and his fate was imminent.

'And hers?' Didi asked a simple question and bit her lip.

Preeti had no real answer.

'There must be someone,' I reasoned. 'A distant relative, an old friend or family on her mother's side . . .'

Preeti cut me short, 'There are many people, but no one who wants to take the responsibility of raising her. Her father is mostly away from the house these days. When he's not working, he's in the hospital. The least I can do is watch over her till he comes home.'

Something changed that day. After that, Didi's visits to Preeti's house grew more frequent as time passed. I never accompanied her again. In fact, she suddenly became so busy that we rarely got a chance to speak despite sharing the same room. She had just started working, so I assumed that the pressure at the office was exhausting her. But her abrupt withdrawal from social life suggested that something more serious was going on. I knew she'd tell me eventually.

One evening, she was already home when I returned from college. I still remember that day vividly. We were sitting on the bed by the window, looking out at our little balcony. The soft evening sunlight shone like streaks in her hair, bathing her face in a tender rosy glow, giving her the aura of something unworldly. I was slightly alarmed because Didi usually came home late from work. She looked tense too, something I scarcely associated with her because I had never seen her worry about anything. Instinctively, I was seized by a feeling of unease and asked, 'What's wrong?'

'There's something I need to do.' She looked tearful and pale. But her voice was resolute.

'You remember Diya?' she asked.

'Diya?'

'The child we met in Preeti's house.'

I listened. I realized that she was not looking for suggestions, nor was she looking for approval or support. She had made up her mind. She was merely asking if I was on her side. It was the only time I think that she truly needed me—the only time it really mattered if I was with her.

I was. But first, I knew that she had the colossal task of breaking the news to our family. She started by telling my mother who initially dismissed the notion as a mere impulse that would go away with time. When she realized how serious Didi was, she called everyone else in the house and they all threw a collective fit.

Didi told them that she had been visiting Diya frequently since we had first seen her. She loved spending time with her, reading and playing with her, taking her out on trips to the museum, the zoo and the amusement park. She said that she had felt a strong connection with the child from the moment she had first laid eyes on her.

She spoke slowly and clearly, trying to pacify the elders in our house and trying to make them understand that although she was just twenty-four years old, she was ready to be a mother to Diya.

'Diya might become an orphan in a year or so. She will either be sent off to live with an unwilling relative or to an orphanage. I have spent a lot of time with the child. She is bright and smart,' she said, 'and deserves better than what will happen to her if I don't intervene.'

Her father and mine were both enraged. 'You are

too young,' they said, 'to throw away your life and future like this. Our society isn't kind and it will certainly not accept an unmarried girl who has a child to take care of. You will remain alone all your life.'

But Didi fought on relentlessly. I knew that in spite of the strong facade she was putting up, her mind was still grappling with uncertainty—not for her own future but for Diya's.

'I'm sure she couldn't ask for a better mother,' I said, because I knew it to be the absolute truth. I tried reasoning on her behalf, but in vain.

Then a welcome break came in the form of a job Didi got as a guest services officer with an international airline. She would be based at Hyderabad airport. Before leaving, she told me that she was pleased about the move. Away from Calcutta, she would be able to keep Diya with her and raise her right. She said that she would take a few months to settle down and then send for the child. She had already spoken to Diya's father and he was only too happy to entrust his daughter to someone who genuinely loved her.

I went to see her off at the airport. We had never been apart and things would not be the same without her.

She walked away, squaring her shoulders, her hair flying behind her. Just as she was about to disappear into the crowd, she turned back and waved. She looked happy, and confident, and hopeful. It was a wonderful moment to remember, for that would be the last time I ever saw her.

Amrita Roy, my sister, died on 5 September 2010 in a freak aerobridge accident in Hyderabad airport while at work.

Diya never went to Hyderabad. But she lives with us now—just as Didi would have wanted. Our parents have grown to love the little angel. She likes mathematics and Enid Blyton and tacos. She's a darling child, though she can be a total brat at times. I try covering up for her as much as I can, though I'm careful not to spoil her. That's what Didi would have asked me do.

The Mysterious Couple

by Rishi Vohra

I had moved back from the US with my family and
we had settled into an apartment in the Lokhandwala
suburb of Mumbai. It was a huge apartment complex;
there were four buildings with fourteen storeys each
and the apartments were frequently sold and bought
because of the escalating property prices. As a result,
we saw many new faces flitting in and out of the lobby
even after six long years.

But there were two faces that had always caught my
wife's and my attention. They belonged to an elderly
couple in their sixties, who were constantly smiling
and seemed to be full of zest for life. They greeted

people who crossed their path, but never slackened the pace of their walk to go beyond that. They always bore a serene expression, kept to themselves, and I never saw anyone visiting them. Usually, I tend to mind my own business, but this couple really piqued my curiosity.

One day, I asked an acquaintance from the society about them. She merely shrugged and said, 'They're weird. They don't talk to anyone. Maybe they are really rich and don't want to mix with our sort.'

Another one said, 'The lady is very nice and has spoken to Mom a couple of times. But when Mom tried to ask details about her, she changed the topic. God knows what trip they're on.'

I casually asked resident after resident about them and got vague and differing opinions. The most extreme one was, 'They are very creepy. I don't even get into the elevator with them.'

As far as I was concerned, there was nothing creepy about them . . . they were just mysterious.

It turned out that the elderly couple lived on the same floor as we did but in a different wing. Our homes were separated by the roughly 6000 square feet of refuge area that was located only on our floor.

Soon, I started spotting the elderly man taking walks in the refuge area every evening; it was a fitting alternative to the building compound on a rainy day. For the first time, I got to observe him at close range. His confident walk and peaceful expression made him look like someone who was enjoying retired life after successfully settling his children on their own paths. But no matter how approachable he looked, I could never muster up the courage to strike up a conversation with him.

One day, when both the elevators in our wing went out of action, my wife and I decided to cross over to the other wing and take the lift from there. Our three-year-old daughter chose to skip ahead and reached the elevator lobby before us.

When we caught up with her, we saw her chatting animatedly with the mysterious couple. They were stuck outside their flat because their door lock had jammed and they were awaiting a locksmith.

We usually don't pull our daughter away from conversations for a reason. She is a very friendly child but chooses whom she wants to talk at length with. And those people are very few. Such lengthy conversations may happen at a store, in the mall, on the street, or even on an airplane. The common thread between all these people, we have noticed, is that she chooses fellow conversationalists who are well-spoken and friendly, irrespective of the strata of society they belong to.

After missing the elevator four times, we took the next ride on the couple's insistence; they realized that we were pressed for time. We offered them assistance with the lock but they politely declined saying that they had just spoken to the locksmith and he was a few minutes away. They were so nice, polite and courteous that I was stumped, given the rumours we had heard about them.

A couple of weeks later, my daughter and I were outside our apartment door receiving a package and we saw the elderly man taking a walk in the adjacent refuge area. My daughter ran to him and after I had signed for the package, I too joined their conversation. Later, my daughter went back inside while I kept chatting with him. He was so intelligent and easy to talk to that all the preconceptions I had of him dissipated immediately.

We started talking about our apartments and progressed into real estate prices, pollution, the city and other such popular topics. When it came to the building society, he mentioned that he didn't really have any friends in the complex, probably because of the fast-paced life that defined most of the residents' lives (almost all the society members were in the age group of below fifty). He seemed oblivious to the gossip behind his back. He went on to relate that he had worked mostly abroad, but had chosen to move back to Mumbai in 1993.

Then the topic shifted to my family and I told him about my background and family. After some time, I asked him, 'Where are your children?'

Suddenly, the cheer evaporated from his face and was replaced by a mask of sadness. He told me that he lost his children in the bomb blasts of 1993. At the time, he was working abroad and his sons were scheduled to visit him. They were at the passport office in Worli submitting the required documents when the blasts had occurred. The last time he spoke to them was when they called him just after they had triumphantly completed all their paperwork and all that was left to do was wait till their stamped passports arrived home. But sadly, their dead bodies beat the passports to it. The boys were in their mid-twenties at the time. To add to the tragedy, the old man's brother-in-law who was roughly the same age as his sons also died with them.

As he gesticulated with his hands to describe the bomb blast, I froze to prevent the tears that collected in my eyes from rolling down my cheeks. He spotted the sadness in my eyes, and immediately retrieved the usual cheer on his face, saying, 'It's all fate.'

He then spoke about his old flat in one of the posh suburbs which had recently gone into redevelopment to pave the way for an upscale society equipped with all the modern and luxurious amenities. He spoke excitedly about moving ahead and avoided talking any further about the devastation that had scarred his life forever.

After our hour-long conversation, I pulled myself away with great difficulty and went home. My neighbour was nothing short of an interesting and endearing man, and I could have conversed with him for hours, but I had already infringed enough on his daily evening walk.

When I entered my apartment, I found my daughter on her bed. I hugged her tightly. Being the affectionate person that she is, she always allows a ten-second hug before she starts trying to escape. But for some weird reason, she let me hug her for several minutes this time. I wondered if she had sensed my pain. But after the hug, she asked me for one of those kiddie scooters. The timing was perfect.

I realized that thanks to my daughter, I had met an amazing and intelligent man whom I would have otherwise never spoken to beyond the customary greeting. Somehow, my little child could recognize the goodness of a person's heart. Maybe all children do. And as adults, we shy away from making friends with, or trying to understand people who are beyond our immediate circle.

I understood the couple's reason for not sharing their personal tragedy with the residents. All they wanted was friendship. Their personal tragedy would have invited only sympathy from others. And they wanted to move beyond it. Since the old man had trusted me with something so personal and painful, I decided to keep it to myself. And I felt somewhat special to be trusted with something so private.

It got me thinking. Had the elderly couple's sons been alive, they would have been well into their forties now, with families of their own. The couple would have experienced all the joys of being grandparents and have so much to look forward to.

Life may not have given them the opportunity to be grandparents to their own sons' children. But life seemed to be giving me the opportunity to give my daughter the grandparents she didn't have from her father's side. I resolved to ask them if my daughter could address them as Dada (Granddad) and Dadi (Grandmom) respectively.

They say that we can only choose our friends but not our family. I say they are wrong. After meeting such remarkable people like Uncle and Aunty, I have learned that there are some people you can choose as family.

How Jhannu Mankdia Made It Possible

by Neelamani Sutar

I am Jhannu Mankdia, the first Mankdia girl child to be a graduate. I am a feature writer, which means that I visit interesting places and write about my experiences. People expect me to steer them to where the sun is blazing hot or maybe to where the snow is powdery soft. They expect me to tell them where to get the best pizza and how not to get cheated while buying souvenirs. The pieces I write are turned into documentary films by the television channel that employs me and are telecast. Sometimes, people send me a letter of praise and when they do so, I get a little more money.

But I have decided to leave my current job. So I'll tell you about my last feature—on my own life story.

Nemiguda, my birthplace, is one of India's many villages and probably one of the poorest. Situated at the foot of some unknown old hills of Odisha, it is home to hundreds of families belonging to the Birhor Adivasi community. As a forest-dwelling society, the Birhor tribes live in the states of Odisha, Chhattisgarh, West Bengal and Jharkhand. It may be noted that the local people call the Birhors by different names. In the districts of Mayurbhanj and Sambalpur, we go by the name Mankdia or Mankirdia. Our community used to kill monkeys and eat their flesh. Perhaps that's why we bear the title Mankdia.

Growing up, life was a struggle for us every single day. Deprived of land, we had to hire ourselves out to make ends meet. Cutting sugar cane, harvesting pulses, going deep into the coal mines, breaking rocks along the roads—we did whatever came our way.

At the beginning of every summer, my father bid farewell to us before setting off with a bundle on his head. Thirty-eight-year-old Sudam Mankdia began his exhausting journey—a week's walk to the palm grove on the shores of the Bay of Bengal. Because of his strong physique, he had been hired by a 'kantarati' (or contractor), a travelling agent who recruited labourers. Working in palm groves required great agility and strength. Men had to climb to the top of the date palm trees barehanded and without a safety harness. These palms were as tall as four- to five-storey buildings. The men had to make a cut in the axil of the palm and collect the milk secreted from the heart of the tree. The acrobatic ascents earned the men the nickname 'monkey-men'. Every evening, the kantarati would come and take delivery of the precious harvest and transport it to a confectioner in Jamshedpur.

We were five children—two brothers and three sisters. I was my parents' third child, my two brothers were much older than me. I was a nine-year-old delicate little girl with long dark hair tied up in two plaits. I had inherited my mother's beautiful slanting eyes. But I had also inherited my father's chiselled nose and thick lips. I had overheard some elders saying that my pointed nose reflected the sharpness of my brain and that the thick lips were a sign of my short temper. I did not wish to attribute such qualities to myself, but I had observed them to be true in the case of my father.

I wore a small gold nose ring, which enhanced the brightness of my face. I got up at dawn, helped my mother with all the domestic chores and went to bed late. I helped closely in raising my two younger sisters—seven-year-old Minnu and five-year-old Sinnu, the two tousle-haired little rascals more willing to kill monkeys and birds than fetching water from the forest brook. Like tens of millions of other Indian children, we had never had the good fortune to go anywhere near a school blackboard. All we had been taught was how to survive in the harsh world into which we were born.

Our small village Nemiguda, though away from the closest bus stop only by some thirty kilometres, was in truth removed from civilization by hundreds and hundreds of kilometres. We, the Mankdia Adivasis, hunted monkeys for food when we did not find anything else to eat. But when the state government banned the killing of monkeys, we lost our reliable source of nourishment. And like all the other occupants of Nemiguda, my family also remained on the lookout for any opportunity to earn the odd rupee.

One such opportunity arose each year at the beginning of the dry season when the time came to pick the tendu leaves that were used to make beedis. For several weeks, my mother and brothers would set off every morning at dawn with most of the other villagers. Their destination was the nearby forest which had quite a few tendu trees. With great precision, they would detach a single leaf and place it in a canvas haversack; they would then repeat the same process over and over again. Every hour, the pickers would stop to make bunches of fifty leaves. If they hurried, they could manage to put together twenty bunches a day. Each bunch was worth the princely sum of two rupees! During the first few days, when the picking went on at the edge of the forest, my mother and brothers would often manage to make around a hundred bunches. My brothers were not quite as skilful as my mother at pinching the leaves off in one go. But together, they usually brought back nearly a hundred rupees each evening—a small fortune for our family that was used to surviving on next to nothing.

One day, the word went round Nemiguda and the peripheral villages that a hockey training school had been set up near the Jharia coal mines in the neighbouring state of Jharkhand. The school would train and educate Adivasi girls in their campus and in return, the girls would work on their farm. People were willing to do anything to bribe the kantarati, who was supposed to be responsible for recruiting the girls. Mothers rushed to the mahajan, the moneylender, to pawn their jewellery and get some money to pay the bribe; if they didn't have any jewellery left to pawn, they chose their only milch cow or a young fleshy male goat.

'My truck will come by four in the morning tomorrow,' announced the kantarati to the parents of the girls he had chosen.

'And when will our children be back?' my father asked on behalf of all the parents.

'Every year during Makar,' the Kantarati responded curtly.

An expression of fear passed over my face. My mother quickly reassured me and said, 'Jhannu, think of what happened to your friend Binita.' My mother was referring to the neighbour's little girl whose parents had sold her to a blind old man so that they could feed their other children.

It was still pitch dark when the truck's horn sounded the next morning. We, the selected girls, were already outside and waiting, huddled together because of the cold. Our mothers had got up even earlier than us to make us a meal wrapped up in sal leaves.

The journey seemed to last quite a while. Eventually, the truck stopped outside a long tiled shed. It was not yet daybreak and the hundred-watt bulb scarcely lit the vast building.

The watchman was a thin bully of a man, wearing a collarless kurta and a lungi. In the darkness, his eyes seemed to blaze like the embers in our chulha.

'All of you, come here and sit down,' he ordered us into a big hall. Then he counted the total number of children and split us into two groups of equal numbers. I was separated from my cousins and sent to join the first group where I saw some unknown faces. Everything seemed so strange. We stayed there for a week.

On the next Sunday morning, a bald man in a black suit arrived at the house carrying two fat briefcases. He held a long conversation with the kantarati. We were not allowed in while he was there, but after he went away, the kantarati came to us, walking very quickly and looking very happy. 'Get ready,' he commanded, clapping his hands, 'the training will start tomorrow.'

They shifted us to another building that same evening and locked us in. Inside the room, I looked around and saw a hideous face staring down at me. The face opened its mouth and growled triumphantly, 'Your duty's over, Mr Kantarati. You may leave now.'

I was frightened. I remember thinking to myself, 'There is no escape for us now! Even if we make a run for it and manage to dodge the men, we still won't be able to get out because the doors are chained! We're done for! Oh Lord, what are they going to do to us?'

The next moment I thought, 'Oh, we have already been sold as indentured labourers. There's nothing left to do. I must leave everything to God and my fate.'

After a few hours, that hideous man loaded us into a truck as if we were poultry birds ready for slaughter. Within half an hour, we found ourselves at Ranchi railway station. A man was waiting for us there. His stern look suddenly terrified me beyond explanation and I began to scream. 'Help!' I shouted, turning my head towards the main entrance in the hope that somebody might hear me. 'Help! Help! H-e-l-p!'

'Grab her!' shouted the bald man. 'Get a hold of her! Stop her yelling!'

Some men rushed at me and then two of them caught me by the arms and legs and lifted me off the ground. I kept screaming, but one of them put a gloved hand over my mouth and silenced me.

The commotion caught the attention of a railway police sub-inspector and he came towards us. The miscreants ran away leaving me there, but the railway police caught them red-handed. The middleman confessed that he was going to sell us in Saudi Arabia. The Ranchi police informed the Odisha police and the next day, we were sent to Bhubaneswar.

Our parents had been informed by then and they rushed to Bhubaneswar to meet us. I embraced my father with tearful eyes.

Later, the Odisha director general of police revealed the whole story in a press conference and praised me. He also requested my father to send me to school. At first, my father was unwilling to do so but finally, he agreed.

The Kalinga Institute of Social Sciences, a Bhubaneswar-based boarding school, adopted me. I started my studies the very next day. I was a wonderful student. I could read, remember what I read, write and recite everything very quickly.

The years flew by and soon, it was time for me to appear for the final examination of the Odisha board. After one and a half months, the board declared our results. I had passed with flying colours.

Now, I am proud to be the first Birhor Mankdia girl to complete my post-graduation. I have decided to open a charitable trust that will educate Adivasi girls. I will encourage the parents from our village, and other villages, to send their children to school. Instead of being known for killing monkeys, I want the Mankdia tribe to learn how to operate computers and become a part of the mainstream workforce, and a part of modern India.

Savita's Story

by Subhobrata

When Savita came to work for us as a domestic help, I was in junior high school. I remember my mother following her from room to room and chatting with her as Savita swept the floors, dusted the furniture and went about other sundry tasks. For Mom, chatting with the maid gave her an excuse to follow her around to make sure nothing went missing. After all, the relationship between a housemaid and her employer often begins with suspicion. For Savita, the small talk killed the monotony of her routine tasks.

What started as a mutually convenient chat soon became something the two women looked forward to. My mom quickly discovered that Savita was a domestic help of a different kind than the ones who had previously worked for her. She was someone who never took shortcuts even when left unsupervised. Meanwhile, Savita discovered a patient listener in my mother, someone who would listen and empathize with a quiet word or two of concern.

Savita stayed in the distant suburbs of south Kolkata. She worked as a domestic help in at least ten households. Every day, she woke up before dawn and reported for work at the first household before six in the morning. To save money, she walked several kilometres from her home to the railway station and back, and travelled in the goods compartment of the train. Her day never ended before midnight. She wore saris discarded by the households she worked in and used every possible honest means to make enough money to cover her family's needs.

In time, we learnt that Savita had an invalid husband at home, who had lost one of his legs in a factory accident. While he was working, he had spent most of his money drinking and his spare time in cussing. That was why they had hardly saved anything. As an invalid without a pension, he spent a large chunk of his wife's income on medicines and most of his time in lamenting about the days gone by.

One would wonder where Savita derived the immense mental strength from to struggle against so many odds. That strength came from her daughter Shanta. Savita was working hard to educate Shanta in a local private English-medium school, because she knew that the quality of education at the government schools was not 'good enough'. Her eyes sparkled with hope and fondness for her child. She was proud of the fact that her daughter had never scored below sixty per cent in any exam. Shanta was among the top ten students of her class, and that too without any tutors, which most of her classmates could afford but she could not.

Savita herself was illiterate. But I can safely say that I have seen very few people in my life who understood the importance of education more than her. She worked hard to pay for the books, school uniforms and other paraphernalia that her daughter's education required. Luckily, she found a mentor in one of Shanta's schoolteachers, who was impressed by her talent and helped her get a scholarship from the school's board of trustees. The scholarship took care of the tuition fees. That was a big relief for Savita because her husband's medical expenses were mounting with his asthma and other physical ailments taking a turn for the worse.

My mother discovered one day that Shanta was just one year junior to me in school. From that time onwards, she preserved my old textbooks and notes and gave them to Savita at the end of the academic year for her daughter to use. Incidentally, this helped me as well. I was accustomed to treating my textbooks with the usual neglect of the privileged class, but I could not bear the thought that the next person who used these books would think of me as a lousy student. So I started caring for my books better and writing my notes more legibly.

At times, during her vacations, Shanta accompanied Savita to work and helped her with some of the strenuous activities such as fetching the cooking water from the municipal tap in the neighbourhood. But the rest of the time, she would sit cross-legged on the floor of our kitchen doing her lessons. My mother often joined in to help with her homework or explain a difficult concept to her. Mom took pleasure in treating Shanta to fruits and other goodies she believed to be healthy for her. Savita reciprocated by running extra errands for us, even though we never asked her to.

In this way, the relationship between Mom and Savita grew deeper over time. It was no longer an employer–employee relationship.

Years passed and Savita's daughter reached the tenth standard. She was ready to give her board exams that year. Savita was certain that her daughter would make her proud. Shanta had topped her class in the pre-board examinations and the schoolteachers had high expectations from her. However, fate had other designs.

A month before her board exams, Shanta fell seriously ill. The doctors diagnosed it as typhoid, but the finding was late, and wrong treatment initially had ensured that her condition had taken a turn for the worse. Savita requested us for some time off. My mother gave her an advance on her salary and some extra cash as well.

Savita's daughter died in the government hospital a day before the board exams were due to begin. We heard the news from her neighbour who also worked in some households in our locality. The neighbour said that Savita had been crying inconsolably, her whole world had come crashing down.

She was back to work after a week. There were dark circles below her eyes, her hair seemed to have greyed overnight, and she was reduced to a shadow of her former self. She did not stop working for us, but she gave up working in many of the other households. She did not need so much money any more, she said, now that she did not have to pay for her daughter's education. But even with the reduced workload, she was visibly emaciated and looked tired and worn out.

From then on, we hardly heard her speak, though she worked as diligently as before. It was as if a mighty stone had set itself upon her chest and squeezed all the vitality, all the laughter and all the joy out of her life.

Years later, when we had moved to a different locality and Savita was no longer working for us, my mother chanced upon her when she visited our old neighbourhood for some work. I was out of college by then and working in a different city; Mom told me the story over the phone.

There was a small store in the neighbourhood that dealt in second-hand textbooks, reference books and the like. When my mother was passing by the shop, she saw Savita purchasing some books from the shop owner. She was much older now and had a slight bend to her spine. Savita recognized my mother and smiled.

Mom stopped to ask her what she was doing there.

'It's for my neighbour's son,' Savita said, and flashed a bright smile at my mother. 'The child is brilliant and is at the top of his class. He wants to be a doctor when he grows up, but his parents are very poor. The boy's father drinks too much and his mother has four other kids to handle. They don't have enough money to pay for his education, so I try to help them by purchasing his schoolbooks, whatever I can afford. Now that I'm alone in this world, what will I do with the extra money I have? What do I have to live for? If this boy gets a good education, he'll be settled in life.'

As my mother's voice crackled across the telephone wires, I could almost see Shanta smiling from the heavens above.

Acid

by Puskhar Pande

I was always against social networking. My idea of being social was meeting people in person. Besides, I frequently read horror stories in newspapers about girls being duped by guys on social websites and was apprehensive about joining one myself. But I had just broken up with my boyfriend and was feeling lonely. Anybody who has been in a relationship knows how awful it can feel when you break up. When I had started dating Mahesh, I had cut off my friendship with most of my classmates. So when we broke up, I was alone and friendless. Mahesh, however, did not suffer much. The last I heard was that he was back to normal after a month of boozing and gaming. I was not. That is how I landed up on an online dating site.

The site I chose asked me to create a profile and provide personal information. After I submitted my details, I got requests from people nearest to my location. Since I was in Mumbai, I got a lot of requests from guys who lived in the city. The site also offered the additional service of online chatting for a designated fee. I subscribed and, as a result, my inbox was flooded with junk emails. I rarely replied to the emails, but I did sign in to a chat room every evening for some light banter. One day when I signed in, I met Himanshu.

Hey, wanna chat?

Yes—I typed back and thus started the endless volley of messages.

So what do you do?

Student, BTech.

Me too—he typed.

Oh, I see. So where are you from?

Mumbai.

I'm originally from Chennai but am studying here in Mumbai.

Cool . . . Listen, I gotta go, my mom is here. Bye.

Bye—I typed, wondering what to make of it.

I visited his profile and saw his pictures. He looked decent enough.

Soon, I received a message from Himanshu asking me to share my email ID so that we could chat. At first I thought of denying his request, but I had liked his profile picture. He was so cute and much better looking than Mahesh.

Late that night, I signed in to my email through my mobile and waited for Himanshu to log in.

My room partner Manali was a bit nosy, so I tucked myself under my quilt to have some privacy. Minutes later, I heard her voice, 'Why are you using the mobile like that—got a new boyfriend or what?'

I peered out from my quilt and saw Manali staring at me with sleepy eyes. The girl was incorrigible. 'No, I just didn't want to disturb you,' I said quickly and turned away from her, pretending to sleep.

She slept soon after and I returned to my cell phone. There were three messages from Himanshu.

Hey. Where are you? Reply if you're there . . .

Hi there! I typed.

Hello, how are you?

Good. And you?

Am good too.

So tell me something about yourself.

I am Himanshu, originally from Madurai but studying here. I live with friends, love travelling and aspire to be an engineer.

What about your parents?

Dad works as an engineer and Mom is a housewife. I have one sister—she is married and settled in Chicago.

Cool—I typed.

What about you?

My name is Prateeksha. I want to do an MBA after completing my BTech. I have one younger brother and Dad has his own business.

But your online profile says that your name is Sumedha. Care to explain?

Such sites are usually not very safe since there are many shady characters out there, so nobody uses their real name.

Oh, but I have uploaded my picture on the site too.

That's okay, you're a boy.

So a boy doesn't have anything to lose? Is that what you're trying to say?

No, but a girl has much more to lose.

Hmmm.

May I see your picture? he typed.

How predictable, I thought. This almost always happened. Most of the boys I met over the Internet asked for umpteen pictures, chatted for a few months and then disappeared all of a sudden. They were looking only to pass the time before they got hitched to a mummy-papa-ki-pasand (Mom and Dad's choice).

Isn't it a bit too early for pictures? I typed back cautiously. I wanted to chat with Himanshu, but I was doubtful about sending my pictures to him. It was common to see morphed pictures of girls on the Internet.

Would you feel less apprehensive if I mailed you mine? he asked.

Yes.

Five minutes later, I received his picture in my inbox.

Where was this taken? I asked.

Australia.

Have you been to Australia?

Yes. I told you I travel.

I hadn't realized he meant international travel. The

guy was obviously rich. And he seemed nice too, but looks can be deceptive. Since he had kept his part of the bargain, I also sent him my picture.

You look good.

Thanks.

Any boyfriends?

Hmmm.

Tell na.

One. We broke up recently.

Why?

Well, because his parents would never agree to our relationship and because he is a liar . . .

There was an awkward silence, and Himanshu went offline. I waited anxiously for him to sign back in. Maybe he was upset by the whole boyfriend thing . . .

Soon, he was back.

Listen, I got to go, but if you like, I can give you my number and we can meet sometime.

Sure.

I sent him my cell number and he sent me his. But the truth was—I was petrified. 'Have I done the right thing by giving away my number so quickly? I know almost nothing about the guy,' I thought.

Two days later, we met. I took the necessary

precautions, informed Manali of my whereabouts, and arranged to meet Himanshu in Barista.

He was really charming. Five minutes into our date, we were chatting away as if we were old pals. We spoke for over three hours and he asked me to be his girlfriend. I mean, who does that on their very first date? Happily, I agreed.

I eagerly told Manali about my new boyfriend because I knew that she would ensure that the news reached Mahesh. 'Wait till he realizes that I have found someone much better-looking than him,' I mused, smiling to myself.

Reached your hostel? Himanshu couldn't refrain from messaging me.

Yes.

Walked?

No, I took a taxi. It is ten kilometres away. Use your common sense, baby.

So I am your baby now?

Yes, I just called you so. I inserted a smiley in my message.

I sent him some pictures, but his demands kept increasing. He now wanted hundreds of pictures of me, each one in a different outfit.

Can you send me one in a skirt?

No.

But why? Am I not your boyfriend?

You are but . . .

But what?

Okay, I will send it at night. My roommate is here right now.

So I sent him the picture at night, and he transformed into the proverbial boyfriend.

Can I kiss you?

Yes, you can.

When?

The next time we meet. Nothing else, not till we get married—I typed, remaining firm.

That's boring.

He kissed me the next time we met and I was happy. We made out a couple of times after that and he tried to take things further, but I didn't let him. I never crossed the limit I had set for myself. The chatting at night continued and gradually, I fell in love with him.

But he continued hinting at sexual advances and I kept ignoring them.

Are you a virgin, Prateeksha? He asked me out of the blue one night.

I did not reply. I was fed up of the sexual overtones that had begun to underline his messages. Suddenly, I realized that he was only interested in sex. It was then that I decided to break up.

You had a boyfriend before, so you must have at least fooled around, right? He persisted.

That's enough. Don't contact me again. It's over—I typed. I was mad and did not want to have anything more to do with him.

What the fuck? You can't break up with me, baby.

I just did.

Then Himanshu began to stalk me. He called and messaged repeatedly, begging me to meet him once. But I remained firm.

I am sorry, sorry, sorry . . . He typed 'sorry' a thousand times in that message, so I relented. And we met.

'Listen, I'm not interested any more. Don't pester me from now on, please,' I said.

'Okay, bye-bye, but there's just one more thing.'

'What?' I asked.

Then he did the unthinkable.

'Take this, you bitch,' he said, and doused me with a bottle full of acid.

There I was—screaming and shouting. My skin was burning and I couldn't see anything. This couldn't be happening! I remember passing out and finding myself awake in a hospital bed.

'Why can't I see anything?' was my first thought. Then it struck me. I had been blinded by the acid. God!

'Am I blind, Mom?' I asked.

'In one eye, dear, or so the doctor says. Your other eye is bandaged.'

'Who the hell was the bastard who did this to you? He won't get away. Just tell me his name,' Papa screamed.

The policemen subjected me to endless questions and comments. 'We've seen many cases like this: girl goes out with boy, when he doesn't land a lucrative job, the girl wants to break up, but the boy doesn't, and this is what invariably happens,' they whispered loudly.

'Is she ready to make a statement?' the policewoman asked. I could barely speak because of the pain and the itching, but I didn't want the bastard to get away. I wanted to see him punished.

'Yes, but please be nice,' my mother pleaded.

'She expects me to be nice to a girl who met with the wrong guy online?' the policewoman sniggered.

I couldn't see anyone, but I could hear it all. After that, I didn't want to make a statement. I just wanted all of them to vanish and leave me alone. But Papa insisted, so I told them everything.

Himanshu was arrested soon after that.

Two months later, I plucked up the courage to look at myself in the mirror. I looked hideous. The doctor told me that the hair wouldn't grow back. Now, every time I went out, I had to cover my face with a dupatta. I looked so ugly. It wasn't fair.

Another month went by and we went to the courtroom. At the hearing, Himanshu showed my messages and said that I had refused to marry him and so he had thrown acid on me out of spite. That was as good as admitting guilt, but strangely, my lawyer didn't pounce on his words. The endless volley of accusations and counter-accusations went on.

'Bail, Your Honour?' his lawyer asked eventually.

'Granted.'

I was shocked. Himanshu was out on bail after just three months.

I contemplated suicide thrice after this, but my mother always managed to call the doctor in time.

'Why me?' I asked myself every night. I used to

love my skin and face. Earlier, people used to look at me because I was beautiful. Now they stared at my face in horror. I was scared to step out of the house.

A few neighbourhood aunties took pleasure in asking me to recount my story again and again. The newspapers printed lies about me saying that I had enticed Himanshu. They even printed the messages that I had sent him.

'Just because I broke up with a boy doesn't mean that he has the right to spill acid on me, does it?' I asked myself and cried over and over.

The best bit came from Himanshu's father. He went on record stating that because I had a boyfriend before, I couldn't be trusted. How could he, as a human being, condone what his son had done?

Meanwhile, the routine visits to the courtrooms turned into an endless charade of counter-questioning.

The verdict was announced five years later: 'Community service and the boy should marry the girl. No cause will be served by keeping him in jail. He has already served enough time.'

My aunt said to me, 'You should consider marrying him, you know.'

But I refused.

No matter what happens, there's always tomorrow.
I will get a job and begin life anew.

An acid attack cannot define me.

Grandparents' Day

by Nalini Chandran

Everyone looked forward to Grandparents' Day at school. I sat in the principal's office on the chair that had brought me such happiness and satisfaction.

I was musing over the years that had gone by when a knock at the door awoke me from my reverie. The peon stuck his head in and said, 'Madam, some people are here to see you!'

'Tell them to come in,' I said, and began clearing my desk of the files I had just finished signing.

A tall, slightly bent and unassuming-looking man with a harassed expression entered. The years had not been kind to him. He stood before me and said,

'Good morning, Madam, I am Ramesh's grandfather. And this is my daughter.'

As his eyes met mine, a shudder went through me and I was catapulted to an evening many years ago—an evening that remained etched painfully in my mind, like a sore that refuses to heal.

I became a widow at the young age of thirty-nine; I had three daughters aged seven, ten and eighteen to raise. My husband had always been my strength and it was very hard to imagine life without him. After the initial days when I almost gave up, I realized that I needed to pull myself together for the sake of the children.

I decided to start a school because I enjoyed teaching: I had taught throughout my husband's career in the army. I also started a spoken English class, which turned out to be quite popular. One of the first poems I taught the young students was Alfred Tennyson's 'Home They Brought Her Warrior Dead'. It was close to my heart because the body of my husband, a colonel in the army, had been brought in honour from Mumbai to his hometown in Kerala.

Being a smart young widow ready to stand on her own, I had to face a number of ordeals soon.

Wagging tongues, slander and anonymous phone calls became regular features of my life. I tried to be brave but the strain started telling on me. I spent many evenings in the bathroom, shedding tears of frustration. But I never let my little ones know the trauma I was going through.

Once, on one of those dreadful anonymous calls, the grating voice on the other side accused me of leading a scandalous life. 'You are running a Youth Centre, aren't you? I've heard that you indulge in some nefarious activities. Is that true?'

'I beg your pardon?'

'You know . . . drugs, prostitution and such temptations for the youth,' continued the unknown caller.

This formed the gist of many such calls from the same caller. Eventually, I started banging the phone down the moment I heard his voice. But the vile calls persisted. I was at the end of my tether.

Finally, I decided to take stock of the situation with the help of my supportive parents-in-law. My father-in-law listened to the whole sordid tale and then came up with a brilliant solution.

When my persistent suitor called next, I purred,

'Look, Mister. You don't seem likely to give up. I am impressed. Why don't we meet?'

'That's an idea. I would love to meet you!' His eagerness was only too obvious.

'But before I meet you, I'd like to know what you do,' I insisted.

He told me his name and added, 'I am a freelance journalist. I was thinking of writing about you and your activities in my newspaper.'

'Please don't! I am a humble widow with three daughters to raise,' I pleaded in true Uriah Heep style.

'Don't worry, dear. Now that you've agreed to meet me, everything is going to be just fine. Tell me, where and when should we meet?'

'Is tomorrow, Saturday, all right with you? You are welcome to come to my house at 7 p.m.'

'Why don't we meet in a hotel? We'll have more privacy there,' he suggested, and the way in which he said this sent a shiver down my spine.

'There's nothing to worry about. I have a fairly decent place with all the necessary facilities.' I dangled the tempting carrot.

The next evening at seven, I heard the creaking

of the gate. A seedy-looking middle-aged man with a receding hairline, paan-stained lips and teeth, and a shabby bag slung over his right shoulder, rang the doorbell.

I opened the door and welcomed him in.

He walked in confidently, looked around appreciatively and remarked, 'Quite an attractive place. Is this your own?'

'Thank God, yes!' I replied. 'Considering my profession, I must keep a pretty place, right?'

Soon, we were talking about trivial things. I oozed as much charm as I possibly could and he fell for it lock, stock and barrel. By the time my eldest daughter brought in some tea and biscuits, my unsuspecting guest was quite at ease. 'Is she your daughter? She's very pretty!' he remarked lecherously.

I smiled provocatively, 'Fortunately, God has blessed me with three girls—ideal for the profession I've chosen.'

'Don't worry, dear. From now onwards, you have a protector in me. I'll be your regular customer.'

'How very nice of you!'

'It's a pity that you have been widowed at such a young age. Your husband was a captain, was he not?'

'No, he was a colonel. Alas, this is my fate! In a society like ours, how else am I to survive?'

Maybe I overdid the histrionics, for he barked, 'Stop whining. A pretty woman like you should have no problem. As I've already told you, I'll look after you.'

'Thank you so much.'

Then he started getting a wee bit restless. 'Shall we proceed to your room?' he said impatiently.

'A little later, if you don't mind,' I replied.

But he stood up with an expression that clearly said, 'Enough of your delaying tactics. Let's get on with what I am here for.'

I knew that my time (or should I say his time) was up. 'All right, Sir,' I said. 'But there's one little ritual left before I entertain you further. I'd like to introduce you to some of my regular customers. I am sure that you'll be interested in knowing some of them, especially since you are a journalist.'

'What are you saying?' he said, thoroughly flabbergasted.

I went to the room next door and shouted, 'Mr B, please come out.'

A white-haired sedate-looking gentleman came out, accompanied by his charming sixty-year-old wife.

Grandparent's Day

'Mr XYZ, please meet Mr B, a retired Supreme Court judge, and this is his wife. Mr B, this is Mr XYZ, a freelance writer.'

Then I went back to the room and repeated the process. In no time at all, my erstwhile tormentor was sweating profusely under the amused scrutiny of eight pairs of eyes—friends of mine from different walks of life. There was a judge, a doctor, a lecturer, a pharmacist and, of course, their respective wives. And then in walked my parents-in-law, their arms akimbo and their invisible 'third eyes' all set to reduce the culprit to ashes.

The wretched villain was almost in tears by now, but I continued my cat-and-mouse game. I purred, 'You said you wanted to write about my nefarious activities. Shall we have the interview now?' As he squirmed, I tormented him further, 'You are welcome to write whatever you want, but if there is an iota of falsehood in your article, I'll sue you.'

The judge put in his bit, 'And I'll take up the case for you, my dear. In fact, why don't we call the police straightaway?' He stood up.

The journalist literally fell at my feet, whining piteously, 'Sister, please don't take this matter to court. Don't call the police. Think of me as your brother.'

My father-in-law spat out, 'Brother indeed! Don't you dare defile my daughter's feet by touching them, you horrible creep! Don't you have a mother, a sister or a wife at home? The next time you blackmail a helpless woman, think of this incident. Now, get lost before you are booted out!'

The skunk quickly slunk out!

And today, many years later, he stood before me—a grandfather who had come to take part in his grandson's annual school programme. He gazed at me and there was a sudden flicker of apprehension and fear in his eyes as the lurid past came alive before his eyes.

But I looked away from him and smiled instead at the mother–son duo that had come along with him. 'Ah, Ramesh, I see that you have brought along your grandfather to see your school and meet the teachers,' I said.

The young mother smiled, 'Oh, he didn't give Father any peace of mind till he agreed to come and meet his principal.'

As if on cue, the little one ran up to me and gave me a hug. 'Yes, Grandpa, this is my favourite teacher and I love her this much,' he said, demonstrating his affection and stretching out his tiny arms.

I reciprocated, 'And I love you too, my baby. Tell me, what kind of a grandfather is he? Does he tell you stories? Of elephants and gods and wicked men who trouble ladies in distress? Of miracles?'

At this juncture, the mother interrupted, 'Oh, my father dotes on Ramesh!'

I lifted the little boy on to my lap, 'You are very lucky to have such a loving grandfather, dear. Now that he is old, there are many things he can learn from you too. I have three daughters and when they were young, their father was taken away by God. So I had a lot of trouble raising them alone. It was people like your grandfather who helped me face life with courage and fortitude.'

I smiled at the old man who sat there with his head bent and tears streaming down his haggard cheeks. Then I told him, 'Don't worry. Your grandson is safe in my hands.'

The Udayan Effect

by Praveen P. Gopinath

In the year 2006, I had finished college and was striving hard to make a living in Dubai. I was going through the worst phase of my life when I met a man named Udayan through a friend. Udayan was working as a delivery boy in a flower shop in Dubai and was earning just 900 dirhams a month as salary. He was almost ten years older to me and used to refer to me as 'aniya', which means younger brother in Malayalam. So I called him 'ettan' or elder brother.

My Dubai visa was going to expire in a few days. I had to stay for at least fifteen more days to get a small payment from a company that I had worked for.

Also, my financial situation was such that I couldn't afford to buy a ticket to fly back to India. To add to my woes, I was on the verge of getting kicked out of the place I was renting. I was desperate for 300 dirhams; that amount would tide me over till I received my payment. But everyone I had asked had refused my request for a loan.

At last, I called Udayan ettan for money, well aware of the fact that his salary was only 900 dirhams, most of which he had to send to his family back in India. As soon as I told him what the problem was, he asked me whether I had enough money to come to Mamzar, the area where he worked. When I kept quiet, he realized that I didn't, so he asked me to take a cab from Sharjah and call him once I reached Mamzar.

As promised, he was waiting for me near the Al Mamzar Centre. He paid for the cab, took me to a nearby cafeteria and after treating me to dinner, gave me the 300 dirhams that I had asked for. He told the owner of the diner that I was his younger brother and that whenever I came there to eat, the owner should write it in his 'pattu book' (a log of credits), which he would settle at the end of the month. He even offered me a bed in the room that he was staying in. But I bid him goodbye and came back to Sharjah.

Fifteen days later, I got my pending payment and on the way to the airport, I went to return the money I had borrowed from Udayan ettan. At first, he kept insisting that I should keep it but at last, he accepted 200 dirhams and told me to keep 100 dirhams if I really thought of him as my elder brother.

Years passed. In 2011, I saw him again standing in front of my shop in Trivandrum. He was searching for me. The old jovial Udayan ettan looked very different now. He had lost his job and was staying at his wife's parents' house with his two kids. When he started speaking to me, I realized that he was a little drunk. He looked at my clothes, smiled and innocently teased me, 'You've made money, aniya. You are rich now.'

I smiled back and a few minutes later we went to the tea shop nearby. As we sipped tea, he shared with me how difficult his life was with no job and an ongoing case at the court. I offered him 1500 rupees, which was roughly equivalent to the 100 dirhams that he had given me then. He accepted the money without hesitation.

A few days later, he came again to the shop, called

me outside and asked me for 500 rupees more. After some more time, he came again and asked for another 1000 rupees. My cousin, friends and staff started noticing the frequent payoffs and told me that the man was exploiting me by calling me aniya.

I don't part with my money if I don't feel like it, and I can easily refuse to give money to even my best friend; but for some odd reason, I could never say no to Udayan ettan. My brain kept telling me that he was exploiting me, but my heart said, 'He gave you 300 dirhams when he earned only 900 himself. He didn't even expect the money back. So even if you are giving him a little money now, it is a far smaller gesture than what he did for you back then.'

In spite of all these justifications, I sometimes got pissed off at him for coming to me drunk and asking for money. He would listen to me like a child and come back a few days later with a five-rupee chocolate or prasad from some temple. My cousin and staff would tease me and say, 'Now here's a man who sells five-rupee chocolates and free sindoor from the temple to you for a thousand rupees.'

Years passed. One day when I reached my shop in the morning, my employee told me that the man who regularly took money from me had come and gone just a few minutes ago. I smiled thinking it was great that I had reached late, otherwise I would have lost some more money.

I sat at the counter and the employee brought me a packet that Udayan ettan had left for me. I saw the square package covered with newspapers and thought that it was probably a packet of biscuits. I wondered if that meant that he was going to ask me for a bigger sum of money. But I was amazed when I opened the packet and found two bunches of 500-rupee notes. There was a total of 1 lakh rupees along with a grimy old piece of paper with writings on it in different colours in Malayalam where Udayan ettan had kept an account of the dates and the amounts he had taken from me. The loan came to a total of 77,350 rupees.

Still reeling, I phoned him and he started giggling. He said, 'I sold my ancestral property near Chempazhanthy for 45 lakh rupees. Today was the registration and I received the entire amount. That's why I came to thank you for helping me and being patient for the last two years.'

'But why did you pay me extra?'

He laughed and told me in his usual tone, 'I am the elder brother and you are my aniya. An aniya can always take money from his elder brother but not the other way round. Go and buy chocolates with the rest of the money. I will come and see you in a day or two.'

He ended the call.

I walked to the bank to deposit the money and thought about how genuine Udayan ettan was. I had assumed that he addressed me as aniya just to be able to borrow money from me; if it were not for his helping me back in Dubai, I would never have helped the man.

He had never told me even once that he was planning to return the money he was taking from me, simply because he didn't consider me any less than his sibling. I always feel proud about my achievements, but that day I felt happier than ever, not because I had got the money back but because a once perfect stranger considered me his own. I felt honoured to be his aniya.

Have you met your Udayan ettan yet? Don't be fooled—they may not be the best dressed or the most well behaved. You can't meet them by design, either. In the most unexpected moment, one day, they will just happen to you.

Time to Pack Up. Not.

by Neha Garg

It was a dazzling Friday evening characterized by the signature Mumbai downpour. The glistening roads and the city lights called out to me. There was a world beyond the four walls of the office that I longed to be a part of. Wrapping up my work for the day, I sighed and thought to myself, 'Time to pack up.'

I left my office around 7.20 p.m. It was still drizzling. I was listening to my current favourite song 'Bahaara' on a loop while I walked to the Khar Road railway station. On the way, I also called my roomie Sakshi and let her know that I would be home in about half an hour. I reached the station and got into the first-class ladies' compartment on a Churchgate slow local. I liked to stand in the moving train and so I took my favourite place at the footboard. There was wind in my hair, water droplets on my face and a Friday evening cheer in my heart.

While I was mentally creating a to-do list for the weekend, I realized that I had forgotten to make an important phone call. I dislike talking on the phone in public places. I thought for a second, 'Maybe I shouldn't make that call right now. I'll reach home and then do it.' But then I changed my mind and called my friend. She did not pick up and I disconnected. As I was about to put the phone back in my bag, a text popped up. I unlocked the phone to read the message, and the next thing I knew I was flying out of the train.

I remember thinking that this was what death must feel like. There were no flashes of my life going by before my eyes, no light at the end of the tunnel and no memory of any faces. It was just a plain boundless void—a sea of nothingness. That split second stretched beyond eternity before I landed hard on the tracks in the middle of nowhere.

I was not dead.

It took me more than a minute to understand where

I was. I saw someone climbing down from the top of an electric pole on the railway tracks and running away with what was probably my cell phone. I was conscious and I thanked the heavens for small mercies.

Slowly, I managed to stand up straight, even though there was no sensation anywhere in my body. I was numb. And petrified. But mostly numb. With unending kilometres of railway tracks stretching in every direction around me, I felt like a headless chicken. Not knowing what else to do, I started to process the information in my head.

A person perched on an electric pole by the railway tracks had pulled me out of the moving train. I had fallen—and I was alive. I had escaped hitting the pole by a few centimetres and the loose rusted iron track grids by a few millimetres. I had lost my phone—and with it, my connection with the world. But I had my handbag with me. My laptop bag was still on the train, which would have already reached my destination station. I could have been home by now. But here I was, all alone on the tracks. I thought about the Kamala Mills rape incident from the previous night, and recalling the phone-snatcher running away in glee, I started to panic. Mumbai was no longer the quintessentially safe city that I had begun to call home. Danger lurked in its dark alleys now, just like in my home city Delhi, the crime capital of India.

Fearfully, I started walking on the tracks. I had to do something, since lying on the tracks waiting for rescue was not a luxury I could enjoy. Soon, I saw a train coming towards me from afar. With no other option in mind, I waved frantically, hoping that the motorman would see me and halt the train. And he did. He asked me what had happened and I narrated the story in broken sentences. He told me to get on the train. Looking back, I still do not remember how I did it. My body was battered and my mind was numb.

I got down at Bandra station, looked for the railway police and informed the on-ground officials about the missing laptop bag. They called the helpline and I was assured that the bag would be found. I just wanted to be done with the whole thing, reach home and fall into a deep slumber. And more than anything else, I needed to feel better. At that time, I did not care about my lost phone or the lost connections any more.

Meanwhile, I learnt that some people from the train that I had fallen from had already reached Bandra station and informed the stationmaster about the incident. A team of police officials had already left to search for me on the tracks. I must admit, in retrospect, that it made me feel special in a perverse kind of way. Till then, I used to think that if I went missing one day, nobody would care. But here were strangers, frantically fussing over a nameless fellow passenger who had been hurt.

As I was telling the officials the whole story, they received a frantic call from the search team saying that they had not found anyone on the tracks. By now the officials had realized that I was the same girl; they called off the search.

They asked me whom I wanted to call, and I was stumped. All my friends' numbers were lost along with the phone. I only remembered my parents' phone number and I did not want to call them. They were sitting thousands of kilometres away and a single phone call from me would be enough to wreak havoc into their peaceful life.

Suddenly, there was a commotion on the platform and I realized that I was its cause. An entourage of railway police officers had come looking for me. I was summoned to the police station, heavily guarded by a convoy. An FIR was registered, the laptop bag was retrieved, and I was ably looked after by a lady constable and a police officer who remained at my side throughout.

Then I was taken to a hospital. At that moment, I felt like an outsider peeping into my own life. I could barely comprehend what was going on and simply watched the agents of the system calmly going about their business.

While waiting for the doctor at the hospital, I rummaged through the contents of my bag in the hope of finding someone's contact information. But it was all in vain. I had no numbers written anywhere. Suddenly, I thought of searching my wallet. There, I found business cards of clients and the odd kirana shop owner. Finally I pulled out my own business card with my office landline number on it. Expecting an office boy to answer, I called up the office, thinking that they may at least send someone to take me home. To my surprise, a colleague answered the call—he was working late. Amidst tears, I managed to tell him enough for him to come running to the hospital in the fifteen minutes with two other colleagues. After numerous tests, X-rays, a sonography and dressings, I was taken back to the police station. I completed a few formalities there and finally, they said that I could go.

I somehow managed to reach home and collapse on my bed.

Everything that could have gone wrong did go wrong that night. And yet, everything fell back into place too. The bruises hurt terribly, but the relief of being alive was a big palliative. The shock of what could have been was great, but the thankfulness for what did not happen was greater. The universe had blessed me in ways that could not be understood rationally.

That night was a second birth for me. It was not my time to pack up yet, after all!

Train to 'Goonda'ville

by Ila Gautam

I was waiting at the crowded Pune railway station for my twenty-year-old daughter Riju to arrive from Mumbai, and I was getting fed up with all the noise. It was nearly 8.30 at night; why was all of Pune at the station at this hour? Logically, I knew that this wasn't really the case, but judging from the people in the crowd moving about aimlessly, it felt like I was at the Kumbh Mela! Even the weather was not suitable for all this gadding about. It was a typical damp July evening, when the rain sometimes got heavier and sometimes confined itself to the usual steady drizzle.

Riju was doing a three-year course in Hyderabad and had been accepted for an internship in Mumbai. Since this was her first weekend in Mumbai and she was so close to home, she had decided to visit us.

We were waiting for the Deccan Queen and my husband Shekhar and I were not unduly worried; the train was considered 'dependable' and was seldom very late. But when the station clock crawled to the expected time and there was still no announcement about its arrival, we were somewhat concerned. We tried Riju's cell phone but consistently got a busy tone. After some time, I told Shekhar, 'Why don't you go and check the status from the enquiry counter— maybe the train is not coming on Platform 1 tonight. I will wait near the exit, just in case.'

While Shekhar was away, I continued trying to contact Riju on her cell phone but with no success. As I was trying for the umpteenth time, suddenly my phone rang. I hastily pushed the ringing sound away from my ear. The screen showed an unknown number. I answered the call, placed the phone back on my left ear and tried to shut out the noise with a finger in my right ear. It was Riju.

'My phone is dead because I had no time to charge

it today. So I have borrowed the phone of a fellow traveller. The thing is, Ma, that our train is stuck at a wayside station called Phugewadi because the track is flooded, and we have been asked to get off the train. What should I do? The train is emptying out. This family travelling with me is going to the makeshift camp. Should I go with them?'

I thought fast, 'Who are these people? Is it safe for her to go with them? And how will we coordinate meeting up with her again if her phone is not working?'

'No, stay in the train—' I started.

But she interrupted me, 'No, everybody is getting down, so it's not going to be safe waiting alone in an empty train.'

I realized that what she was saying made sense. 'Right. You will be safer in a public place. Go to the bus stand in Phugewadi. We will look for it and get to you as fast as we can. Don't move from there—or how will we find you?' I cautioned her just before the line went dead.

Shekhar returned at the tail end of the conversation and I told him everything after the call got disconnected. He had also received the same information from the enquiry counter, but with the valuable addition of where exactly the track had been flooded to bring the train to a standstill. We were somewhat new to Pune, so we had no idea where Phugewadi, or the Deccan Queen, or our daughter was.

We rushed out as fast as it was possible to walk in the crowded, wet, muddy and slippery conditions. We reached the car and got in, breathing a sigh of relief. Shekhar, who was driving, quickly manoeuvred the car out of the crowded streets in the immediate vicinity of the station.

The rain was still coming down relentlessly. Even with a fast windscreen wiper, the road was barely visible in the dark. Away from the noisy station, I noticed the empty roads. Indeed, who would be walking about at such a late hour in the pouring rain? Shekhar was a steady driver as a rule, but we were both worried now and he was already driving our Maruti 800 abnormally fast. The road conditions were far from good—the rains had resulted in some serious potholes. It was a bad ride, but we barely noticed it, what with the worried silence in the car. At one point, we stopped to ask for directions and were told in precise detail where we should go. So we headed towards the university.

It was getting very late, and having recently come from Delhi, I was worried about a young, unaccompanied girl being out on the streets at this hour. Kidnap, murder, rape—my mind was racing through the worst possible scenarios even as I was trying to tell myself that all would be well. After all, we were in Pune now, where I had begun to realize things were very different from the way they were in Delhi.

I broke the silence to ask, 'That man said that we had to go straight for only for about two kilometres on this road. Haven't we done that already?'

'No, not yet,' my husband gave me a terse reply and fell back into silence.

I remember getting angry at Riju. 'Why is she so careless? She doesn't even bother to keep her phone charged! What is the point of having a cell phone when you can't use it when you need it the most? Emergencies don't give you a call beforehand to tell you that they are going to arrive! When I meet her, I will scold her like there's no tomorrow. Such an irresponsible girl!' But I was also praying fervently in my heart, 'Oh God, please keep my daughter safe! Where is she? What's happening around her?' Illogically enough, I thought that if I concentrated on Riju and sent her all my mental energy, she would be protected.

After we had crossed a particular bridge, I felt that the directions and landmarks we had been given were not matching with what we saw around us. I turned to Shekhar and asked, 'That man said that we will get a road on the right but I can't see such a road. Are we going in the right direction?'

Too worried to argue, Shekhar agreed with me. 'I was also wondering,' he said.

There were very few passers-by as we drove on. We were convinced that we were on the wrong road, but what should we do now?

Then we saw two young men walking hurriedly in the same direction that we were going. We stopped to ask them for fresh directions. One exclaimed, 'Oh, you are on the wrong road! Take a U-turn and cross the bridge again to the other side of the Mula river. Then go back till Bremen Chowk and from there take the road to the right.'

Oh God! It was already so late and now, we would have to go back quite a way to get on the right road. I asked hopefully, 'Isn't there a shortcut from here?'

The young man regretfully shook his head and said, 'No, you'll have to go back.'

We had no other option, so we thanked them, turned around and started the drive back to Bremen Chowk. I dared not look at my watch any longer. We reached the Chowk after what seemed like an eternity, took the right road and sped onward silently into the gloomy unknown along the barely visible road.

Suddenly, our headlights picked out a sign that said 'Phugewadi'. At last! But there were no passing vehicles or any people around whom we could ask for directions to the bus stand. However, we spotted a group standing under a dim streetlight in the distance on the opposite side of the road. There were a few men and a young woman. And I instantly knew it was her!

There she was under an umbrella, surrounded by three or four young men. How vulnerable she looked! Those uncouth ruffians were clearly hovering around her to tease or harass her, or maybe even worse . . . There was a slum on the other side of the road; it was obvious that the boys were from there. And I was the one who had insisted that she wait at such a place! Still, she was alive and no Ravana had carried her away. Yet.

We made a quick U-turn and screeched to a halt near her. Surely the boys would melt away now that we were there. But cheekily, they continued to stand right where they were!

Then I got the shock of my life when Riju turned around, handed the umbrella to one of the boys, smiled and said something to him.

Had she lost her mind? Why was she talking to them? Didn't she know that only encouraged them? I hastily opened the door for her, willing her to move quickly to safety. She got in the car and I exhaled my first deep breath in a long, long time.

On the drive back home—this time at a more sedate pace now that our precious child was safe with us—we asked Riju to explain her peculiar behaviour. She said, 'When I reached the bus stop, I found that it was only a "by request" stop; there was no one there. I stood and waited for a long time. Then these boys came up to me and asked me why I was standing there. I told them why. Then one of them said, "Why don't you wait in my house over there and my mother can look after you. You will be safe and also more comfortable out of the rain." I declined and said, "But how will my parents recognize you? I need to wait here at the bus stop." Then he gave me his umbrella and said, "Okay then, we will wait here with you, since it is not safe for you to wait here alone." That is why they were standing with me till you arrived.'

Hearing her words, I was deeply ashamed and moved. Here I was, with my preconceptions about slum boys, and all along they had been standing in the rain to protect my daughter! How horribly wrong of me! My judgement was based on bias and outward appearance. I am glad to say that that day a responsible group of boys changed my way of thinking and replaced my mistrust with a new faith in the decency of human beings.

What Goes Around Comes Around

by Tulika Dubey

It was a cold morning in Muzaffarpur when young Nagina got a piece of news that crushed his heart. Newly appointed as a lecturer in the Lalit Narayan Mithila University in Darbhanga, Nagina had befriended a fellow lecturer named Amish and had begun to consider him almost like family. The two friends were to start their planned journey to Patna soon for the most important interview of their lives. But when Nagina reached Muzaffarpur on the pre-decided date, he was informed that Amish had already left for Patna three days ago.

Nagina didn't take long to decipher what had happened. Cold despair gripped his heart as he realized that his best friend had deceived him in order to get an edge over him in the interview.

Just a week ago, the Bihar Public Service Commission had announced that they would be conducting an interview to recruit a permanent lecturer at the LNMU. Nagina and Amish were both temporary recruits and the BPSC announcement signified a life-changing opportunity. So the two friends had applied for the same position. While Nagina had realized that he would be competing with his best friend, his simple heart had failed to foresee that Amish would gladly forfeit their friendship and do whatever it took to get ahead. That's why when Amish proposed that they meet in Muzaffarpur one day prior to the interview and take the ferry to Patna together, Nagina had gladly agreed.

The fact that Amish had left for Patna three days ago meant only one thing—he had been lobbying in the academic circles and contacting key members to ensure his selection. For Nagina, who was an outsider and didn't know anyone at a higher rank to help his cause, this was the end of the world.

With a heavy heart, he took the ferry to Patna alone, feeling dejected and hopeless.

At exactly 8 a.m. the next morning, Nagina reached the venue dressed in his most immaculate formals. He made sure that his exterior did not betray his shattered confidence. Finally, when his name was called for the interview, he found himself in front of an intimidating panel. The BPSC chairman, Mr Ram Shukla, was flanked on either side by senior experts. Their grim faces and disinterested demeanour extinguished what little hope Nagina was left with.

After a few moments of awkward silence, Mr Shukla suddenly asked him an unexpected personal question, 'Where are you from, Mr Dubey?'

Nagina was startled. He thought this might be a test to examine his communication skills and tried to cram all the information he could into one sentence, 'Sir, I am from a remote village called Bandanwar in the Godda district which is . . .'

'Bandanwar?' Mr Shukla interrupted him.

Nagina didn't think anyone would know the name of his tiny village. He was not sure if Mr Shukla, bored of the interview, was attempting to amuse himself by disconcerting him or if he had genuinely developed a sudden interest in his village. Either way, the question had nothing to do with his interview.

Nagina glanced at Mr Shukla again. There was something different now in his eyes. They sparkled with a childlike curiosity and Nagina could sense desperation when Mr Shukla asked him the next question, 'Do you know Kanti Prasad Dubey?'

Nagina was lost. Why was the BPSC chairman asking him if he knew his grandfather? He swallowed and nodded, 'Yes, Sir, he is my grandfather. He is bedridden now because of old age.'

And there in the midst of the stoic interview panellists, the unfeeling dark interiors and the intimidating hall, Nagina saw Mr Shukla's eyes fill with tears as he exclaimed, 'But he is alive! Will you do me a favour? Will you tell him I said pranam and that I seek his blessings?'

For the young man who was seated there in the hopes of securing a permanent post, this was a little too confusing. He merely nodded.

The rest of the interview passed in a flurry as the panellists were already awed by the boy who had managed to make the chairperson cry. They asked a few standard questions and he answered them.

Nagina walked out of the room satisfied with his performance.

The results were announced and to everyone's surprise, Nagina Dubey was recruited to the sole permanent post of lecturer at the university. It was the happiest day of his life.

Amish could not understand how an outsider who didn't even belong to this side of the state had succeeded despite his lobbying. For Nagina, it was one of the first victories of life. His credentials were already impeccable; he was a gold medallist and had passed his master's course with a first class. But this victory restored his faith in God. Not only did it mean that he had the mettle but it also meant that no one could cheat anyone out of something they deserved. Little did he know that the reason for a part of his victory at least came from the distant past, something that happened a long time before he was born.

After a year at his new job, Nagina visited his village and met his bedridden grandfather, Kanti Prasad Dubey. He had grown thin and frail and his eyes were blank now, tired of life. Sometimes, he didn't speak for days on end. It was obvious that he was waiting for death to arrive. Nagina was told that his grandfather had lost most of his hearing, and it was then that it occurred to him to tell his grandfather about the interview. Nagina slowly repeated most parts of the story several times, but in the absence of any reaction from the old man, he could not guess if his grandfather had understood anything.

But things changed in a trice when Nagina uttered the name of Ram Shukla. The old man's hand moved sharply and he turned to look at Nagina. 'Say that name again?' his voice cracked. It was the first time he had spoken in days.

'Ram. Ram Shukla.'

'Ram?' he repeated, and for the first time in his entire life, Nagina saw his ninety-year-old grandfather cry.

Since his grandfather refused to talk any more, Nagina sought out his eldest uncle to see if he knew anything—and finally, he learnt the whole story.

Thirty-five years ago, Kanti Prasad Dubey was appointed the principal of a school in a village named Bhabhua. He had to live away from family and could see them only once a month, but he was disciplined and loved his work.

One day in the middle of the school year, a bright boy called Ram Shukla came to his office with a sad face. His parents had informed him that he needed to drop out of school since they could not afford the hostel and school fees any more. Kanti pondered over the problem for a day and came up with a solution. He invited Ram to live in his own quarters for free, which took care of his food and lodging needs. Kanti also decided to pay the child's school fees out of his own pocket.

It was a dream come true for Ram. Not only did he learn from his master in the classroom, but he also got special tuitions at home and absorbed a lot simply by sharing a roof with his principal. Out of gratitude, he ran errands for his teacher and helped with odd jobs around the house. Meanwhile, Ram filled a gap for Kanti, who was away from his family. Over the years, teacher and pupil developed a strong bond. And when Ram completed his matriculation, he bade his teacher goodbye; that was the last they saw of each other.

After thirty-five years, the student and the teacher had heard about each other for the first time through Nagina. When his uncle finished the story, Nagina realized that he had played only a small part in a beautiful karmic story. He had served to bring Ram

Shukla an opportunity to reach out to his long-lost teacher and to bring peace to his grandfather. Today, as his grandfather lay on his bed ready to leave the world, he had heard a story which had brought him peace—his dear student had not forgotten him.

Kanti Dubey smiled just a little and closed his eyes forever, content in the knowledge that what goes around does come around.

It Fell in a Storm

by Santanu Bhowmick

I love the raw power of a storm. It is one of the most spectacular shows of nature and when it passes, it leaves behind a light that is nothing short of magnificent. That was why I went for a walk after the storm. The dark skies were enchanting, the clear air smelled wonderful, the leaves on the trees seemed freshly washed and the water drops on them looked like they were just about to fall but they didn't—they just hung there, shining like little Christmas lights, making the trees look like Christmas trees.

In the middle of my walk, I saw some children running away from an angry old man. He was screaming and shouting at them, and the two boys and a little girl scampered across the street like rabbits, dragging a bag behind them. I didn't know what the matter was and didn't care to investigate. I kept walking and watched the kids disappear into a lane.

A few minutes later, I saw the children again. They were collecting mangoes that had fallen on the streets from the trees in the storm. I understood now why the man had been angry at them: they were probably after the mangoes that had fallen from his tree. I used to do the same thing in my childhood—the only difference was that the children were collecting mangoes from the streets and my friends and I went into the forest to collect them. So we didn't have any angry old men chasing us.

I watched the children as they went from one mango tree to another. One of the kids soon realized that I was observing them. He got a little nervous for a moment but then he decided to ignore me and kept picking the mangoes off the street.

I walked up to them and asked, 'What are you doing?'

Startled, the two boys said nothing but the little girl said elatedly, 'We are collecting mangoes.'

The two boys, probably her elder brothers, didn't approve of her talking to me. 'Why do you ask? Are you going to tell the owners?' queried one of the boys.

'No, why would I do that? You are collecting mangoes that have fallen on the street. It's not like you are stealing them from somebody's tree,' I replied, hoping that siding with them might break the ice.

It did.

'Try telling that to the old man who just chased us,' said the other boy.

I smiled and they kept collecting the mangoes.

Not all the mangoes were in good shape. After all, they had fallen from the trees on to the concrete. Some of them were bruised, some had cracked open and others had split right into two. The children inspected each mango they found. If it was any good, they put it in their bag; if not, they threw it away and moved on to the next tree and the next until it was time to move on to the next street.

I was also walking along with them, though I maintained a healthy distance so that nobody would associate me with them. I was worried that if another old man came out of his house and chased them, the children would run away quickly—but where would that leave me? It would be rather embarrassing for me if I were caught as one of their associates. So I was careful not to get so close that I might not plausibly deny any involvement with the children if accosted. Meanwhile, I realized that the kids had started trusting me; they knew that I wouldn't tell on them because if I had wanted to, I would have done so already.

Suddenly, the little girl noticed that the guava trees had also relinquished their fruits during the storm, and she started picking these up as well. She inspected each one for bruises and cracks and put them in the bag or threw them away.

Time passed and as we went from street to street, I found myself entrusted with the role of the lookout. I didn't know when this assignment happened but I was happy to go along with the idea, as long as it didn't get me into trouble. I must admit that we had some close calls and I secretly enjoyed the little element of danger. It reminded me of my younger days, but for a gentleman like me to be seen mingling with street urchins in this task was a little awkward. So I made every effort not to be seen with them, especially by someone who knew me. It was not a problem to talk to them or walk with the children while they went from street to street but when they did the actual picking, I stayed clear of them.

I looked at their bag and realized that they had more than enough for themselves and yet, they were searching for more fruits. I noticed another strange thing—they hadn't eaten a single mango or guava from the bag. I clearly remembered that while on jaunts like this in my childhood, my friends and I would put some mangoes into a bag, eat some of them and throw the half-eaten mangoes all over the forest, but these kids were doing none of that.

'Don't you think you have enough mangoes for yourselves?' I asked.

They looked at me but said nothing. After a moment, the little girl said, 'We are not collecting them for ourselves; we are going to sell them.'

One of the older brothers promptly elbowed her. It was evident that they did not want to disclose their plans to me.

After a while, when the boys went a little further to pick the mangoes, the little girl walked up to me slowly and told me their secret.

'We are going to sell these mangoes so that we can buy a gift for our mother. Today is her birthday. We spent all morning thinking about what we could give her, but we had no answers until the storm hit. Then one of my brothers came up with the idea of picking up the fallen mangoes and selling them to get the money for her gift.'

I was impressed by the diligence of the kids to show their mother how much they loved her. And yet, the nostalgia and my reflection of childhood was shattered by that one hard blow of reality.

The little girl went back to join her brothers to inspect and pick up the mangoes, and I stood there processing the information I had just received. I could not believe how fast things could change. A moment ago these kids looked happy, excited and cheerful; they were an image of the spirit of universal childhood. But now, the same kids looked sad and gloomy: an epitome of the reality that most of us don't see or prefer not to, and even go so far as to ignore them when images like these are thrust in front of us.

They were young children. The oldest was probably ten years old and the younger boy maybe eight; the little girl couldn't be more than six. This was not the age to collect mangoes to sell in the market to earn money to buy their mother a birthday gift—but what could I do? If I offered them money, that would be insulting—not only to them but also to their cause. So I did nothing and simply walked along.

After some more streets and a lot more mangoes and guavas, the children decided that they had enough and went towards the market. I had been with them till now in their journey so I decided to stay a little longer and watch the culmination of their efforts.

They knew that they couldn't sell the fruits in the market itself because the permanent shop owners would object, so they decide to set up shop on the street side on the way to the market. I watched them as they put down the bag on the side of the road, poured the contents on to the grass, neatly divided the mangoes and guavas according to their quality and size and then stacked them carefully on the bag. There were two main piles—one for the guavas and one for the mangoes. The guava pile was more or less consistent but the mango pile had fruits of many types and sizes. It was an odd mix and thus their prices were low but still, people bargained with them. I wondered how people could haggle with such small children. I felt disgusted and sorry for the people who bargained, but not for the children. In my eyes, the children were heroic.

The fruits sold quite quickly due to their cheap price. Only a few mangoes remained now—they were so few that people didn't even stop to look at them. The kids were quite anxious to sell the last of their stock as soon as possible, understandably so because they needed the money to buy the gift for their mother and the day was almost bordering on evening.

I decided to step forward and offered to buy them all. 'Okay, I need some mangoes too. How much are these?'

The little girl smiled at me and the boys started calculating. Then they said, 'Eight rupees.'

I took out a ten-rupee note and gave it to them. Instantly, they started to fumble in their bag to give me change.

'Don't worry, keep the change,' I said, but they refused to listen to me and gave me a two-rupee coin.

'So, have you decided what gift you want to buy for your mother?' I asked.

The boys glared at their sister—it had been their secret and she hadn't been able to keep it to herself.

At that moment, I felt like I had betrayed her trust. It was awkward.

Finally, one of the boys said, 'We haven't decided yet. We will count the money and then see what we can afford.'

They poured out all their money on the bag and counted it; it was a little over a hundred rupees. By the looks they exchanged, it was obviously more than they had expected. Then the deliberations started on what they should buy. The three of them didn't make any meaningful progress for a long time, until the little girl spotted an umbrella salesman. He was wandering on the rain-soaked streets, looking for his next client.

'Ma could use an umbrella. She always comes home soaking wet,' suggested the little girl. Her brothers agreed.

I stood there watching them as they ran towards the umbrella salesman and started sifting through different patterns and colours, but the little girl was fixated on a beautiful white umbrella with red flowers all over it.

She pointed to it and said, 'I want that one.'

But that particular umbrella was out of their price range. No matter how much the umbrella salesman tried to explain that to her, she wouldn't understand. Then her brothers joined in and tried their best to convince her otherwise, but how does one argue with a six-year-old child who is on the verge of tears?

I couldn't just stand and watch any more.

The children were facing the umbrella salesman and had their backs towards me. I pulled out a fifty-rupee note from my pocket and waved it at the umbrella salesman. He glanced at me. I placed my finger on my lips and gestured for him to be quiet too. He understood what I meant. He gave them the umbrella and took whatever money they gave him.

As the children went on their way with their gift, the umbrella salesman slowly walked up to me, took the fifty-rupee note from my fingers and walked away.

I know that many would call what I did 'charity', but it wasn't. I think it was the children who were charitable to me. What is the value of money anyway but the paper it is printed on? What really gives money its value is the need that someone has for it. For me, the value of a fifty-rupee note is a chocolate bar, or maybe a bag of chips, or a plate of noodles; but to those kids, that same fifty-rupee note was a way to show their mother the appreciation they had for her love and care. They had just increased the value of my fifty-rupee note a million fold, for who knows how their mother might have reacted when she got her birthday gift? She might have cried, and it would be sacrilege to put a price on those tears of joy.

After that day, I looked for those children whenever I walked past the market, hoping never to see them selling fruits by the side of the road again.

I never saw them again.

An Encounter of a Special Kind

by Tapan Mukherjee

My father was a medical professional working for a private company in Raniganj in West Bengal. The officers of the company were housed in individual bungalows inside a large campus. Our house was in a corner of the campus. The officers' club was adjacent to the boundary wall of our garden; its premises were reminiscent of the British Raj with a series of high-ceilinged rooms and a common veranda in the front. The compound was luxurious with green grass, colourful flowers and a host of tall and majestic trees. The seasonal vegetables in the kitchen gardens of the households and the magnificent trees constantly attracted many species of birds and squirrels; a group of langurs had even made their den in an ashwatha tree nearby. They had all become a part and parcel of our existence and daily life. I never failed to wonder at the dexterity of a squirrel in manipulating a nut or a berry and the untiring and highly skilled nest-building of a tiny sunbird.

There are certain incidents from our childhood that leave a permanent mark on us and continue to subtly influence our life. A small incident on a Saturday afternoon left a profound effect on me and unfolded before my eyes a whole new dimension to the wonders of God's creation.

It was a few days into the Puja vacation. Just like for any other child, the holidays provided an opportunity for me to become engrossed in various magazines and storybooks published specially for children in the festive season.

After a hearty lunch, my parents and my younger sisters lay down for an afternoon nap and I settled down with a storybook. The quiet afternoon presented the perfect backdrop for reading an adventure story. The silence was occasionally broken by the sound of my family snoring, the intermittent chirping of house sparrows, the harsh cawing of a crow and the shrill call of a kite flying high above the ground. Minutes ticked by. I became deeply absorbed in the book.

Suddenly, I heard a group of street dogs barking furiously in the distance. I chose to ignore the commotion thinking that the pack of dogs might have cornered a hapless pig. But soon, the barking became louder and more aggressive and the alarmed cawing of a flock of crows added to the cacophony. I also heard the disturbance approaching closer. Curiosity got the better of me. Leaving the book aside, I rushed to the veranda to see what was going on.

I glanced towards the roof of the club house and saw something horrible. A big male langur, apparently the leader of its group, was holding a baby langur in his hands and mercilessly biting it all over with a definite intent to kill. Meanwhile, a pack of stray dogs had gathered on the ground and were barking away at their natural foe sitting on the roof while a flock of crows was cawing continuously and circling overhead. The helpless mother of the baby and other lesser members of the langur group were scattered on the roofs of the buildings nearby watching the baby being killed. I recalled the terrible custom in the animal clan according to which a dominant male usually does not allow another male baby or adult to survive within its group.

Without losing any time, I gathered a stout stick in one hand and hurled a piece of stone at the marauding langur. The langur was so infuriated that it hardly took any notice of my assault. But then I started throwing more stones. The dogs on their part raised their pitch of cry.

The changed circumstances and the sudden unexpected attack from unknown quarters forced the langur to drop the baby from the sloping roof over the veranda. The baby was listless and appeared to be dead. As its body started to slide down, the excitement of the pack of dogs grew manifold at the prospect of a good kill and meal. Keeping the dogs at bay with the stick, I managed to catch hold of the baby langur's tail just as it tipped over the edge of the tiled roof. The baby appeared inert and lifeless. It was indeed a male baby.

By this time, my parents and sisters had come out on to the veranda and were witnessing my rescue operation. Some of our neighbours had also gathered in the distance.

I took the baby langur to our backyard and gently laid him on the floor inside the poultry coop. His body was full of deep bite marks and scratches. Blood was oozing from some of the wounds. The baby remained motionless. My father provided first aid to clean the wounds and stop the bleeding. I was relieved to find out that the baby was breathing, even though his breaths were shallow.

Splashes of cold water made the baby stir and after a few shaky attempts, he sat up. He was in state of shock and started trembling like a leaf in the wind. His two little twinkling eyes welled up with tears and he started to sob with a muffled cry—just like a human child would after experiencing trauma. I offered him a peeled banana which he accepted with his unsteady hands and began taking hesitant bites.

My attention was fixed on the revival of the baby langur. Suddenly, I had an uncanny feeling of being watched. I turned away from the coop and looked up. There sat the mother langur on our kitchen roof, watching every move I made. She simply sat there quietly, as if convinced that no harm was being done to her child.

Meanwhile, the baby sensed the presence of his

mother and started to sob and cry a little louder. I retreated from the door of the coop to allow the mother access to her baby.

Immediately, the mother descended on the floor of the coop and picked up the baby in her arms. She gave the baby a thorough body inspection to check his injuries and then cuddled him tightly in her bosom. The baby found great solace in her caring arms. The mother sat still with the baby in her lap for a few minutes. It was almost as if she was pondering over her options and trying to figure out how she could keep the baby safe from further assault.

For a few seconds, the mother langur looked straight into my eyes. Even today, I cannot forget that look in her eyes, showering silent gratitude on me for saving her child. I was overwhelmed by the emotion, the sentiment and the way she said thanks to me. There sat a universal mother holding a stricken child in her lap.

Then, in a flash, she jumped with her baby clinging to her belly and reached our kitchen roof. She surveyed the area for the vicious male langur and then leapt away in the direction opposite to the place of the violent encounter.

That brief meeting with the mother and the baby langur convinced me that interspecies communication and mutual trust is indeed a reality and should anyone strike the right chord, the relationship hums into action. The mother langur showed me that food was not the only means of communication between man and animal but that there were other means of establishing a bond through trust, compassion and mutual understanding.

That realization has driven me to look around my small world and seek pleasure in the company of various life forms—whether it is a sapling of a shy 'touch-me-not' plant or a baby snake or a tiny ashy prinia foraging under the bushes for food.

Fifty-five years have passed since that day. I am now seventy years old. But I still fondly remember that 'encounter of a special kind'.